2006

no

now
R.U
!

Sherri

The *Ultimate* RV Cookbook

BORN 2 RV

Recipes for the Traveling Chef

Copyright © 2005 CQ Products
Waverly, IA 50677
All rights reserved.
No part of this book may be reproduced or transmitted in any form
or by any means, electronic or mechanical, including photocopying,
recording or by any information storage and retrieval system, without
permission in writing from the publisher.

Printed in the United States of America
by G&R Publishing Co.

Distributed By:

507 Industrial Street
Waverly, IA 50677

ISBN 1-56383-195-3
Item #7006

Table of Contents

How to Use This Cookbook:

The Ultimate RV Cookbook can truly make your next voyage more enjoyable by providing all the information you need to make main dish recipes for Breakfast, Lunch and Dinner while you're on the road.

Each chapter in this cookbook begins with a shopping list. From that shopping list you can prepare and serve three days worth of meals, that is, Breakfast, Lunch and Dinner for three entire days. Look over the shopping list before you leave home, as there may be some ingredients you already have on hand, such as some of the spices, butter or "others" that are required.

Also, remember to pack extra airtight containers, as they are often needed to hold leftovers for following meals. Look for the * or ** within each recipe and read the corresponding directions at the bottom of the recipe, as these are important tips and instructions. In some cases extra "tools" are needed, such as aluminum foil, non-stick cooking spray or a hand mixer.

Most importantly, drive safe and have fun as you explore the world around us!

Trip One

SHOPPING LIST

Dairy & Eggs:
- ❑ 1 stick butter
- ❑ 4 C. shredded mozzarella cheese
- ❑ 3 C. shredded Cheddar cheese
- ❑ 3 C. milk
- ❑ 1 small can grated Parmesan cheese
- ❑ 1 small container cottage cheese
- ❑ 10 eggs

Fruits & Vegetables:
- ❑ 3 onions (1 small)
- ❑ 3 cloves garlic
- ❑ 1 large bunch broccoli
- ❑ 6 large carrots
- ❑ 1 (4 1/2 oz.) can sliced mushrooms
- ❑ 6 stalks celery
- ❑ 1/2 C. raisins
- ❑ 2 small green bell peppers
- ❑ 4 large potatoes
- ❑ 1 small bunch green onions

Meats:
- ❑ 8 boneless, skinless chicken breast halves
- ❑ 2 1/2 lbs. ground beef
- ❑ 1 pkg. sliced pepperoni
- ❑ 8 slices bacon

Breads & Grains:
- ❑ 1 (12 oz.) pkg. mini lasagna noodles
- ❑ 2 C. uncooked white rice
- ❑ 1 (9") unbaked pie crust
- ❑ 3 C. quick oats
- ❑ 4 hamburger buns

Spices, Oils & Sauces:
- ❑ Salt & Pepper
- ❑ Paprika
- ❑ Cinnamon
- ❑ Garlic powder
- ❑ Dried rosemary
- ❑ Chicken bouillon granules
- ❑ 1 (1 oz.) env. dry onion soup mix
- ❑ 1 small bottle vegetable oil

Others:
- ❑ 3/4 C. sugar
- ❑ 2 T. brown sugar
- ❑ 3 (10 3/4 oz.) cans cream of mushroom soup
- ❑ 1 (10 3/4 oz.) can cream of celery soup
- ❑ 1 (10 1/2 oz.) can French onion soup
- ❑ 1 (16 oz.) can pizza sauce
- ❑ 1 T. baking powder

Breakfast
Day One:

Easy Cheesy Quiche

Makes 6 servings

3 T. butter, melted, divided
1 onion, minced
1 tsp. minced garlic
2 C. fresh chopped broccoli
1 (9") unbaked pie crust
1 1/2 C. shredded mozzarella cheese
1/2 C. shredded Cheddar cheese
4 eggs, well beaten
1 1/2 C. milk
1 tsp. salt
1/2 tsp. pepper

Preheat oven to 350°. In a large saucepan over medium low heat, place 2 tablespoons butter. Heat until butter is melted and add minced onion, minced garlic and chopped broccoli. Cook slowly, stirring occasionally, until softened. Transfer broccoli mixture to unbaked pie crust and sprinkle with shredded mozzarella and Cheddar cheese. In a small bowl, beat together eggs and milk. Season with salt and pepper and stir in remaining 1 tablespoon melted butter. Pour egg mixture over ingredients in pie crust. Bake in oven for 30 minutes, or until center of quiche has set.

Lunch
Day One:

Broccoli & Carrot Lasagna

Makes 6 servings

2 C. chopped broccoli
2 carrots, chopped
1 (12 oz.) pkg. mini
   lasagna noodles
1 (10 3/4 oz.) can cream
   of mushroom soup
1/4 C. plus 1/8 C. grated
   Parmesan cheese, divided

1/3 C. cottage cheese
1 1/2 C. shredded
   mozzarella cheese,
   divided
1/2 tsp. garlic powder
1/2 tsp. dried rosemary,
   crushed
1 tsp. paprika

Preheat oven to 375°. In a small pot of water or vegetable steamer over medium heat, steam broccoli and carrots until tender. Fill a medium pot with water and bring to a boil over medium high heat. Add half of the box* of lasagna noodles and cook until softened. In a separate bowl, combine cream of mushroom soup, 1/4 cup Parmesan cheese, cottage cheese and 1 cup shredded mozzarella cheese. Mix well and set aside 3/4 cup of the mixture. To remaining mixture, add garlic powder, dried rosemary and steamed broccoli and carrots. Mix well and set aside. To assemble, in an 8x8" pan, layer half of the vegetable mixture and cover with half of the cooked lasagna noodles. Top noodles with remaining half of the vegetable mixture, followed by the remaining half of the noodles. Top with reserved 3/4 cup cheese mixture. Sprinkle with remaining 1/2 cup shredded mozzarella cheese. Combine paprika and remaining 1/8 cup Parmesan cheese and sprinkle over mozzarella. Cover pan with aluminum foil and bake for 30 minutes. Remove aluminum foil and bake for an additional 10 minutes.

*Reserve remaining noodles in package for Lunch and Dinner on Day 3.

Dinner
Day One:

Chicken Rice Casserole

Makes 4 servings

1 (10 3/4 oz.) can cream
of mushroom soup
1 (10 3/4 oz.) can cream
of celery soup
1 C. water
1 C. uncooked white rice
1 (4 1/2 oz.) can sliced
mushrooms, drained

Pinch of garlic powder
Pepper to taste
1 (1 oz.) env. dry onion
soup mix
8 boneless, skinless
chicken breast halves

Preheat oven to 325°. In a large bowl, combine cream of mushroom soup, cream of celery soup, water, uncooked rice, drained mushrooms, garlic powder and pepper. Mix until well incorporated. Spread mixture evenly into a 9x13" baking dish. Lay skinless, boneless chicken breast halves over soup mixture in baking dish. Sprinkle onion soup mix over chicken and cover dish tightly with aluminum foil. Bake in oven for 1 to 1 1/2 hours, until chicken is cooked throughout and no longer pink. Remove four of the cooked chicken breast halves, wrap and store in refrigerator.*
*Reserve leftover cooked chicken for Dinner on Day 3.

4

Breakfast
Day Two:

Hash Brown Breakfast Sandwich

Makes 5 servings

4 large potatoes, peeled and quartered
8 slices bacon
1 C. shredded Cheddar cheese

4 eggs, beaten
2 T. vegetable oil
Salt and pepper to taste

Fill a large saucepan or pot with water and place over medium high heat. Add peeled and quartered potatoes and bring to a boil. Continue to boil until potatoes are tender, about 5 minutes. Drain pot and run potatoes under cool running water. Drain potatoes and pat dry. Using a shredder or grater, grate potatoes into a large bowl. Divide shredded potatoes into two even sections and place each section on a separate piece of waxed paper. Pat each section of potatoes into a 6" circle. In a medium skillet over medium high heat, cook bacon until browned. Remove bacon to paper towels to drain and drain skillet of fat. Set aside 4 slices of the bacon.* Cook eggs in skillet until lightly scrambled and remove to a plate. Add oil to skillet and reduce heat to medium. Place remaining 4 slices of bacon, scrambled eggs and shredded Cheddar cheese over one of the hash brown patties. Using the waxed paper to pick it up, flip remaining hash brown patty over patty with bacon, eggs and cheese to make a large sandwich. Place the entire sandwich in heated skillet and cook until browned on one side. Using a large spatula, carefully turn over entire sandwich and cook until remaining side is brown. To serve, cut breakfast sandwich into wedges.

*Reserve 4 slices cooked bacon for Lunch.

Lunch
Day Two:

Cheddar Bacon Burgers

Makes 4 burgers

**Leftover cooked bacon
   from Breakfast
1 lb. ground beef
1/2 C. shredded Cheddar
   cheese**

**1/2 tsp. salt
1/2 tsp. pepper
1/2 tsp. garlic powder
4 hamburger buns**

    Crumble leftover slices of bacon from Breakfast into small pieces. In a medium bowl, combine ground beef, drained chopped bacon, shredded Cheddar cheese, salt, pepper and garlic powder. By hand, mix well until fully combined. Shape mixture into four hamburger patties. Preheat grill or place burgers in drained skillet over medium high heat. Cook burgers for 5 minutes per side, until fully cooked to desired doneness. Place one burger on each hamburger bun.

Dinner
Day Two:

French Onion Bake

Makes 6 servings

1 lb. ground beef
1 C. uncooked white rice
1 (10 1/2 oz.) can French
onion soup
1 (10 3/4 oz.) can cream
of mushroom soup

2 stalks celery, chopped
1/2 C. chopped green
onions
1/2 C. chopped green
bell pepper

Preheat oven to 350°. In a lightly greased 2-quart casserole dish, combine ground beef, uncooked rice, French onion soup, cream of mushroom soup, chopped celery, chopped green onions and chopped green bell peppers. Mix all together until thoroughly combined. Cover baking dish tightly with aluminum foil and bake in oven for 1 hour.

Breakfast
Day Three:

Baked Raisin Oatmeal

Makes 8 servings

1/2 C. vegetable oil	1 T. baking powder
3/4 C. sugar	3 C. quick oats
2 eggs	1/2 C. raisins
1 C. milk	2 T. brown sugar
1/2 tsp. salt	1/2 tsp. cinnamon

In a medium bowl, combine vegetable oil and sugar. Stir in eggs, milk, salt, baking powder and oats. Mix until well incorporated and fold in raisins. Pour mixture into a lightly greased 9x13" baking dish. Sprinkle brown sugar and cinnamon over mixture and cover tightly with aluminum foil. Chill in refrigerator for 30 minutes. Preheat oven to 350°. Bake oatmeal in oven about 35 minutes, until firm. To serve, spoon hot oatmeal into bowls.

Lunch
Day Three:

Chicken Noodle Soup

Makes 6 to 8 servings

**Leftover cooked chicken
   from Dinner Day One**
**4 carrots, peeled and
   chopped**
4 stalks celery, chopped
**1 large onion, peeled
   and chopped**

8 C. water
Salt and pepper to taste
1 tsp. chicken bouillon
**Leftover mini lasagna
   noodles from Lunch
   Day One**

Cut cooked chicken into small pieces. In a large soup pot, combine chicken pieces, chopped carrots, chopped celery and chopped onions. Add water to cover chicken and vegetables. Bring mixture to a simmer, adding a little more water if needed. Crumble half of the remaining uncooked lasagna noodles to desired size.* Add crumbled noodles to pot and heat until softened, about 8 to 10 minutes. Add salt, pepper and chicken bouillon. Mix well until heated throughout. To serve, ladle soup into bowls.

*Reserve remaining half of the leftover uncooked noodles for Dinner.

Dinner
Day Three:

Pizza Casserole

Makes 6 to 8 servings

Leftover mini lasagna
noodles from Lunch
Day Three
1/2 lb. ground beef
1 small onion, chopped
2 cloves garlic, minced
1 green bell pepper,
chopped

1 small pkg. sliced
pepperoni
1 (16 oz.) can pizza sauce
4 T. milk
1 C. shredded mozzarella
cheese

Preheat oven to 350°. Crumble remaining mini lasagna noodles to desired size. In a pot of lightly salted water over medium heat, cook noodles for approximately 6 to 8 minutes, until al dente. In a medium skillet over medium heat, sauté ground beef and chopped onions, minced garlic and chopped green bell pepper. Heat mixture until ground beef is cooked throughout and vegetables are softened. Drain skillet of fat and stir in drained cooked noodles, sliced pepperoni, pizza sauce and milk. Mix well and pour mixture into a lightly greased 2-quart casserole dish. Bake in oven for 20 minutes. Remove from oven and sprinkle shredded mozzarella cheese over casserole and return to oven for an additional 5 to 10 minutes, until cheese is melted.

Trip Two

SHOPPING LIST

Dairy & Eggs:
- ❑ 1 stick butter or margarine
- ❑ 10 eggs
- ❑ 1 small jar mayonnaise
- ❑ 1/2 C. milk
- ❑ 2 1/2 C. shredded Cheddar cheese

Fruits & Vegetables:
- ❑ 1 small can refried beans
- ❑ 1 head romaine lettuce
- ❑ 3 large tomatoes
- ❑ 2 onions
- ❑ 2 green bell peppers
- ❑ 1 lemon
- ❑ 1/3 C. chopped celery
- ❑ 1 large red apple
- ❑ 2 (14 1/2 oz.) cans French-cut green beans
- ❑ 1 (4 oz.) jar diced pimento peppers

Meats:
- ❑ 16 slices bacon
- ❑ 3 (1 lb.) flank steaks
- ❑ 6 boneless, skinless chicken breast halves
- ❑ 1 (6 oz.) can tuna

Breads & Grains:
- ❑ 12 (10") flour tortillas
- ❑ 2 C. seasoned croutons
- ❑ 8 split English muffins
- ❑ 1 C. uncooked wild rice
- ❑ 1 (16 oz.) pkg. uncooked spaghetti

Spices, Oils & Sauces:
- ❑ Garlic powder
- ❑ Salt & Pepper
- ❑ Ground ginger
- ❑ Cinnamon
- ❑ 1 chicken bouillon cube
- ❑ 1/4 C. soy sauce
- ❑ 2 T. distilled white vinegar
- ❑ 1 small bottle vegetable oil

Others:
- ❑ 1/4 C. brown sugar
- ❑ 3 T. honey
- ❑ 1 small jar peanut butter
- ❑ 1 (10 3/4 oz.) can cream of celery soup
- ❑ 1 (10 3/4 oz.) can cream of chicken soup
- ❑ 1 (8 oz.) can water chestnuts

Breakfast
Day One:

Breakfast Burritos

Makes 4 servings

16 slices bacon
4 eggs
1 small can refried beans

1/2 C. shredded Cheddar cheese
4 (10") flour tortillas

In a medium skillet over medium high heat, cook bacon until crispy. Remove bacon and let drain on paper towels. Set aside 8 slices of bacon.* Drain skillet of fat. Wrap the tortillas in aluminum foil and keep warm in a 100° oven. Crack eggs into drained skillet and scramble lightly with a fork while cooking. Meanwhile, in a small saucepan over medium low heat, place refried beans. Cook until heated throughout, stirring occasionally. To serve, spread an even amount of the heated refried beans over each heated flour tortilla. Top with 2 strips of bacon, some of the scrambled eggs and some of the shredded Cheddar cheese. Fold and roll tortillas like burritos and serve.

*Reserve 8 slices cooked bacon for Lunch.
**Start marinating steak for Dinner (see page 14).

Lunch
Day One:

B.L.T. Salad

Makes 4 to 6 servings

Leftover cooked bacon
   from Breakfast
3/4 C. mayonnaise
1/4 C. milk
1 tsp. garlic powder
1/8 tsp. pepper

Salt to taste
1 head romaine lettuce,
   rinsed and torn
2 large tomatoes, chopped
2 C. seasoned croutons

Crumble leftover slices of bacon from Breakfast into small pieces. In a medium bowl, using a whisk, combine mayonnaise, milk, garlic powder and pepper. Whisk thoroughly until blended and smooth. Season to taste with salt. In a large serving bowl, combine torn romaine lettuce, chopped tomatoes, and crumbled bacon. Toss until well incorporated. Pour dressing over salad and toss until evenly coated. Sprinkle croutons over salad and serve.

Dinner
Day One:

Easy Marinated Steak

Makes 4 servings

1/4 C. soy sauce
3 T. honey
2 T. distilled white vinegar
1/2 tsp. ground ginger

1/2 tsp. garlic powder
1/2 C. vegetable oil
3 (1 lb.) flank steaks

In a medium bowl, using a whisk, combine soy sauce, honey, vinegar, ground ginger, garlic powder and vegetable oil. Whisk thoroughly until fully blended. Lay steaks in a shallow baking dish and pierce all sides of each steak with a fork. Pour marinade mixture over steak, turning steaks to coat both sides. Cover baking dish tightly with aluminum foil and marinate steak in refrigerator for 6 to 8 hours. Preheat grill or place a large skillet over medium high heat. Lightly oil the grate or skillet and place marinated steaks on the grill or in the skillet. Discard the marinade. Grill steaks for 10 minutes, turning once, until completely cooked to desired doneness. Remove one of the fully cooked steaks, wrap and refrigerate.*
*Reserve cooked steak for Dinner on Day 3.

Breakfast
Day Two:

Veggie Omelet

Makes 2 to 4 servings

2 T. butter, divided	**4 T. milk**
1/2 onion, chopped	**3/4 tsp. salt**
1 green bell pepper,	**1/8 tsp. pepper**
** chopped**	**1/2 C. shredded Cheddar**
6 eggs	** cheese**

In a medium skillet over medium heat, melt 1 tablespoon butter. Add chopped onion and chopped green bell pepper and sauté until vegetables are tender, about 4 to 5 minutes. Meanwhile, in a medium bowl, beat together eggs, milk, 1/2 teaspoon salt and pepper. Remove sautéed vegetables from skillet and transfer to a separate bowl. Sprinkle remaining 1/4 teaspoon salt over vegetables. Return skillet to medium heat and add remaining 1 tablespoon butter. Melt butter and spread to coat skillet. Pour egg mixture into hot skillet. Heat for about 2 minutes, until egg mixture begins to set at the bottom of the pan. Gently lift edges of egg and push inward so the uncooked part of the egg mixture flows toward the edges. Continue to cook until the center of the omelet starts to look dry, about 2 to 3 minutes. Sprinkle shredded Cheddar cheese over omelet and spoon sautéed vegetables over cheese. Using a spatula, carefully fold one edge of the omelet up and over the cheese and vegetables. Cook omelet for an additional 2 minutes, or until cheese is melted. Slowly slide omelet onto a plate and divide into portions.

Lunch
Day Two:

Simple Tuna Melts

Makes 4 servings

1 (6 oz.) can tuna, drained
1/3 C. chopped celery
2 T. mayonnaise
Pinch of salt

4 English muffins, split
1 tomato, sliced
1 C. shredded Cheddar
   cheese

Lightly toast each English muffin half. Preheat broiler or preheat oven to 350°. In a medium bowl, combine drained tuna, chopped celery, mayonnaise and salt. Mix well and spread tuna mixture evenly over the 8 English muffin halves. Place 1 slice of tomato over tuna on each muffin and sprinkle an even amount of the shredded Cheddar cheese over each tomato slice. Place tuna sandwiches on a baking sheet and place in oven or under broiler. If using broiler, heat for 3 to 5 minutes, until cheese is melted. If using oven, heat for 5 to 7 minutes, until cheese is melted. Place two tuna melts on each of four plates and serve.

Dinner
Day Two:

Easy Tetrazzini

Makes 4 servings

1 (16 oz.) pkg. uncooked spaghetti
6 chicken breast halves
1 (10 3/4 oz.) can cream of chicken soup

1 C. water
2 T. butter
1 chicken bouillon cube
1/4 C. shredded Cheddar cheese

Preheat oven to 350°. In a medium pot of lightly salted water over medium heat, place spaghetti. Bring to a boil for 6 to 8 minutes, until spaghetti is al dente. Meanwhile, in a large skillet over medium high heat, heat chicken breast halves until cooked throughout and no longer pink. Remove cooked chicken from saucepan and chop into small pieces. Place half of the cubed chicken in an airtight container and place in refrigerator.* Drain cooked spaghetti and spread evenly in the bottom of an 8" square baking dish. Place remaining half of the chopped cooked chicken over spaghetti. In a medium saucepan over medium heat, combine cream of chicken soup, water, butter and chicken bouillon cube. Bring mixture to a boil and pour over spaghetti and chicken in baking dish. Sprinkle shredded Cheddar cheese over mixture and press down lightly. Bake in oven for 25 minutes.
*Reserve cooked chicken for Lunch on Day 3.

Breakfast
Day Three:

Sweet Breakfast Rounds

Makes 4 servings

1/2 C. peanut butter	1/4 C. brown sugar
4 English muffins, split	2 T. butter or margarine
1 large apple, cored and sliced	1/4 tsp. cinnamon

Lightly toast each English muffin half. Spread 1 tablespoon peanut butter over each toasted English muffin half and top each with some of the apple slices. In the small microwave-safe bowl, combine brown sugar, butter and cinnamon. Heat mixture in microwave until melted. Stir mixture and drizzle lightly over each serving. Place two rounds on each of four plates and serve.

Chicken Spectacular

Makes 6 to 8 servings

3 C. water
1 C. uncooked wild rice
Leftover cooked chicken
    from Dinner Day Two
1 (10 3/4 oz.) can cream
    of celery soup
1 (4 oz.) jar diced pimento
    peppers, drained

1/2 onion, chopped
2 (14 1/2 oz.) cans French-
    cut green beans, drained
1 C. mayonnaise
1 (8 oz.) can water
    chestnuts, drained
    and chopped
Salt and pepper to taste

In a medium saucepan over medium heat, combine water and wild rice. Bring to a boil, reduce heat, cover and let simmer for 50 minutes, or until rice is tender. Preheat oven to 350°. In a large bowl, combine cooked rice, leftover cooked cubed chicken from Day 2, cream of celery soup, drained pimentos, drained green beans, mayonnaise, chopped water chestnuts, salt and pepper. Mix well and pour into a 9x13" baking dish. Bake in oven for 25 to 30 minutes, or until heated throughout.

Dinner
Day Three:

Steak Fajitas

Makes 4 servings

Leftover cooked steak from Dinner Day One	**1 green bell pepper, cut into thin strips**
2 T. vegetable oil	**1 lemon**
8 (10") flour tortillas	**Salt and pepper to taste**
1 large onion, cut into thin strips	

Cut leftover cooked steak from Day 1 into thin strips. In a large skillet over medium high heat, heat 1 tablespoon vegetable oil. Wrap the tortillas in aluminum foil and keep warm in a 100° oven. Add steak strips and cook until fully heated. Remove steak strips from skillet, set aside and keep warm. To skillet, add remaining 1 tablespoon vegetable oil and strips of onion. Cook until onions are softened and add strips of steak and green bell pepper. Squeeze the juice of the lemon over ingredients in skillet and stir until fully combined. Season with salt and pepper to taste. Serve mixture with heated tortillas.

Trip Three

SHOPPING LIST

Dairy & Eggs:
- ❑ 1 1/2 C. shredded mozzarella cheese
- ❑ 1 stick butter
- ❑ 8 eggs
- ❑ 1 C. liquid non-dairy creamer
- ❑ 1/2 C. milk

Fruits & Vegetables:
- ❑ 8 cloves garlic
- ❑ 2 (14 1/2 oz.) cans green beans
- ❑ 1 small piece gingerroot
- ❑ 3 small onions
- ❑ 1 (14 1/2 oz.) can diced tomatoes in juice
- ❑ 1 (14 1/2 oz.) can chopped stewed tomatoes
- ❑ 5 green bell peppers (4 large)
- ❑ 2 (4 oz.) cans sliced mushrooms
- ❑ 1 small tomato

Meats:
- ❑ 6 boneless, skinless chicken breasts
- ❑ 3 (1 lb.) pork tenderloins
- ❑ 2 lbs. ground beef

Breads & Grains:
- ❑ 8 hamburger buns
- ❑ 1 (14 oz.) tube refrigerated pizza crust dough
- ❑ 2 C. white rice
- ❑ 3 C. quick oats

Spices, Oils & Sauces:
- ❑ Salt and Pepper
- ❑ 1 small bottle white cooking wine
- ❑ Dried onion flakes
- ❑ Cinnamon
- ❑ Garlic powder
- ❑ Lemon juice
- ❑ Liquid smoke flavoring
- ❑ Steak sauce
- ❑ Ground mustard
- ❑ Olive oil
- ❑ Paprika
- ❑ Garlic salt

Others:
- ❑ 1 small bottle ketchup
- ❑ 3/4 C. prepared mustard
- ❑ 2 tsp. cornstarch
- ❑ 1/4 C. chicken broth
- ❑ 1/2 C. cashews
- ❑ 1 1/4 C. brown sugar
- ❑ Honey
- ❑ 1 3/4 C. apple cider
- ❑ 3/4 C. flour
- ❑ 1 1/2 tsp. baking powder
- ❑ Non-stick cooking spray
- ❑ Cider vinegar
- ❑ 1 1/2 tsp. Worcestershire sauce
- ❑ 1 (10 oz.) bottle soy sauce

Breakfast
Day One:

Cinnamon Oat Pancakes

Makes 4 servings

2 T. butter
2 T. cider vinegar
1 tsp. cinnamon
1 3/4 C. apple cider

1 C. quick oats
3/4 C. flour
1 1/2 tsp. baking powder
2 eggs

Preheat griddle or place a large frying pan over medium heat. Lightly oil the griddle or pan. In a medium microwave-safe bowl, place butter. Heat butter in microwave until melted and add cider vinegar, cinnamon, apple cider and oats. Mix well and return bowl to microwave for an additional 2 minutes. In a separate bowl, combine flour, baking powder and eggs. Add flour mixture to oats mixture and stir well. To make pancakes, pour 1/4 cup of the oat mixture onto the hot griddle or into the frying pan. Cook until pancake is browned on both sides, flipping once. Repeat with remaining batter.

Lunch
Day One:

Pulled Chicken Sandwiches

Makes 4 servings

6 boneless, skinless chicken breasts	5 T. honey
1 1/2 C. ketchup	1/4 C. steak sauce
3/4 C. prepared mustard	4 T. lemon juice
5 T. brown sugar	3 T. liquid smoke flavoring
6 cloves garlic, minced	Salt and pepper to taste
	4 hamburger buns

In a large skillet or saucepan over medium high heat, place chicken breasts. Heat until chicken is cooked throughout and no longer pink. Meanwhile, in a medium saucepan over medium heat, combine ketchup, mustard, brown sugar, minced garlic, honey, steak sauce, lemon juice and liquid smoke flavoring. Bring to a low boil, reduce heat and let simmer for about 10 minutes. Season with salt and pepper to taste. When chicken is cooked throughout, remove from skillet and chop or shred into pieces. Place chopped chicken in saucepan with sauce mixture and stir until heated and well combined. When mixture has cooked throughout, remove half of the chicken mixture and place in an airtight container and set aside.* To serve, spoon remaining chicken mixture onto hamburger buns.

*Reserve leftover chicken mixture for Dinner on Day 2.
**Start marinated pork for Dinner (see page 24).

Dinner
Day One:

Marinated
Pork Tenderloin

Makes 4 servings

1/4 C. soy sauce	1 tsp. cinnamon
1/4 C. brown sugar	2 T. olive oil
2 T. white cooking wine	Pinch of garlic powder
1 1/2 tsp. dried onion flakes	3 (1 lb.) pork tenderloins

In a large ziplock bag, combine soy sauce, brown sugar, sherry, dried onion flakes, cinnamon, olive oil and garlic powder. Close bag and shake until well mixed. Place pork tenderloins in bag, seal and place in refrigerator for 4 to 6 hours. Preheat grill to medium high heat or place a large skillet over medium high heat. Lightly oil the grate or skillet. Place marinated pork tenderloins on grill or in heated skillet. Discard the marinade. Grill or cook tenderloins for 15 to 20 minutes, or to desired doneness, turning once. Remove one of the cooked tenderloins, wrap and place in refrigerator.* Slice remaining two pork tenderloins in half and serve.

*Reserve cooked tenderloin for Dinner on Day 3.

Breakfast
Day Two:

Sweet Oatmeal

Makes 4 servings

3 3/4 C. water
2 C. quick oats
Pinch of salt
4 tsp. butter

8 T. brown sugar, divided
1 C. liquid non-dairy
    creamer
4 T. milk

In a medium saucepan over medium heat, bring water to a boil. Reduce heat to low and stir in quick oats and salt. Cook until oats have thickened, about 3 to 5 minutes. In the bottom of each of four serving bowls, place 1 teaspoon butter and 1 tablespoon brown sugar. Spoon hot oats into each bowl and stir until butter and brown sugar are melted. Pour 1/4 cup liquid creamer and an additional 1 tablespoon brown sugar over each serving. Mix lightly and serve.

Stuffed Green Peppers

Makes 4 servings

2 C. uncooked white rice
2 small onions, chopped
2 lbs. ground beef
1 (14 1/2 oz.) can diced
    tomatoes in juice

1 (14 1/2 oz.) can chopped
    stewed tomatoes,
    drained
Salt and pepper to taste
4 large green bell peppers

Preheat oven to 325°. In a medium pot, cook white rice according to package directions. When rice is cooked and tender, remove half of the cooked rice to an airtight container.* In a large skillet over medium heat, place ground beef and chopped onion. Heat until onions are softened and ground beef is fully cooked. Remove half of the cooked onion and ground beef mixture and place in an airtight container in refrigerator.** Keep remaining half of the ground beef and onion mixture in skillet over medium heat and add remaining half of the cooked rice. Add diced tomatoes with juice and half of the chopped stewed tomatoes.*** Mix well and season with salt and pepper to taste. Meanwhile, cut tops off of the green bell peppers and scoop out the seeds and flesh. It may be necessary to slightly slice the bottom of each pepper so the peppers can stand up. Fill each pepper with a generous amount of the rice and ground beef mixture. If desired, top peppers with green pepper tops that were cut off. Place filled peppers in a 9x13" baking dish. Bake in oven for 20 minutes, or until peppers reach desired tenderness.

*Reserve cooked rice for Dinner on Day 3.
**Reserve cooked ground beef mixture for Lunch on Day 3.
***Reserve remaining half of the chopped stewed tomatoes for Lunch on Day 3.

Dinner
Day Two:

BBQ Chicken Pizza

Makes 4 servings

**Leftover chicken mixture
from Lunch Day One**
**1 (14 oz.) tube refrigerated
pizza crust dough**

**1 C. shredded mozzarella
cheese**

Preheat grill to medium heat or oven to 350°. In a medium saucepan over medium heat, place leftover chicken mixture from Day 1. Cook until mixture is heated throughout, about 3 minutes, being careful not to boil. Meanwhile, spread pizza crust dough evenly onto a 10" to 12" pizza pan. Spoon heated chicken mixture over pizza crust. Sprinkle shredded mozzarella cheese over pizza. If using grill, cover grate with aluminum foil and spray non-stick cooking spray over the foil. Remove pizza from pan and place dough with toppings directly on aluminum foil. Grill until dough is hardened, being careful not to burn, and cheese is melted. If using oven, bake pizza in the pan for 15 to 20 minutes, until crust is lightly browned and cheese is melted.

Breakfast
Day Three:

Veggie Scrambled Eggs

Makes 4 servings

1/4 C. olive oil
2 (4 oz.) cans sliced
   mushrooms, drained
1 small onion, chopped
1 green bell pepper,
   chopped

6 eggs
1/4 C. milk
1 small tomato, chopped
1/2 C. shredded mozzarella
   cheese

Chop the onion, tomato and green bell pepper. Set aside half of the chopped green bell peppers.* In a large skillet or frying pan over medium high heat, place olive oil. Add drained mushrooms, chopped onions and remaining half of the chopped green bell pepper. Sauté until vegetables are tender. In a medium bowl, using a whisk, combine eggs and milk. Add egg mixture to vegetable mixture in skillet and stir in chopped tomatoes. Heat, scrambling with a fork, until eggs are almost set. Stir in shredded mozzarella cheese and heat until cheese is melted and eggs are fully cooked.

*Reserve half of the chopped green bell pepper for Lunch.

Lunch
Day Three:

Super Sloppy Joes

Makes 4 servings

Leftover ground beef mixture from Lunch Day Two
2 T. ketchup
Leftover chopped stewed tomatoes from Lunch Day Two
Leftover chopped green bell peppers from Breakfast
1 T. brown sugar
1 1/2 tsp. cider vinegar
1 1/2 tsp. Worcestershire sauce
1 1/2 tsp. steak sauce
1/4 tsp. garlic salt
1/8 tsp. ground mustard
1/8 tsp. paprika
4 hamburger buns

In a large saucepan, place leftover ground beef and onion mixture from Day 2. Cook until mixture is heated and stir in ketchup, leftover chopped stewed tomatoes from Day 2, leftover chopped green bell peppers from Breakfast, brown sugar, vinegar, Worcestershire sauce, steak sauce, garlic salt, ground mustard and paprika. Continue to cook, stirring frequently, until mixture is simmering and heated throughout. To serve, spoon mixture onto hamburger buns.

*Start marinating pork for Dinner (see page 30).

Dinner
Day Three:

Cashew Pork Stir-Fry

Makes 4 servings

Leftover pork tenderloin
**   from Dinner Day One**
1/4 C. soy sauce
2 tsp. cornstarch
2 (14 1/2 oz.) cans green
**   beans, drained**
2 tsp. olive oil

1 small piece gingerroot,
**   minced (about 1 T.)**
2 cloves garlic, minced
1/4 C. chicken broth
Leftover cooked rice from
**   Lunch Day Two**
1/2 C. cashews

Cut leftover pork from Day 1 into small pieces. In a medium bowl, combine soy sauce, cornstarch and chopped pork. Cover bowl and chill in refrigerator for 4 hours. In a large skillet over medium heat, place olive oil. Add minced gingerroot and minced garlic and sauté for 1 minute. Add pork mixture with liquid to skillet and cook for 1 1/2 minutes, stirring constantly. Stir in drained green beans and continue to cook until mixture is heated throughout. Stir in chicken broth, reduce heat and let simmer for 2 minutes. In a microwave-safe bowl, heat leftover cooked rice from Day 2 in microwave for about 1 minute. To serve, place heated leftover rice on serving plates and spoon stir-fry mixture over rice on each place. Sprinkle cashews over each serving.

Trip Four

SHOPPING LIST

Dairy & Eggs:
- ❑ 1 (12 oz.) can evaporated milk
- ❑ 9 eggs
- ❑ 3 C. milk
- ❑ 1 1/2 sticks butter
- ❑ 1 C. mayonnaise
- ❑ 1 C. sour cream
- ❑ 3 C. shredded Cheddar cheese
- ❑ 2 C. ricotta cheese
- ❑ 1 C. shredded mozzarella cheese
- ❑ 1/2 C. grated Parmesan cheese

Fruits & Vegetables:
- ❑ 2 onions
- ❑ 1 green bell pepper
- ❑ 1 (4 oz.) can sliced mushrooms
- ❑ 1 head broccoli
- ❑ 1 (14 oz.) can sauerkraut
- ❑ 1 (10 oz.) pkg. frozen chopped spinach

Meats:
- ❑ 1 (16 oz.) pkg. ground sausage
- ❑ 8 boneless, skinless chicken breast halves
- ❑ 2 T. bacon bits
- ❑ 3 lbs. ground beef

Breads & Grains:
- ❑ 1 tube of 8 refrigerated buttermilk biscuits
- ❑ 1 (10" to 12") prepared pizza crust
- ❑ 2 C. crushed cornflakes
- ❑ 1 small loaf crusty bread
- ❑ 10 to 12 manicotti shells
- ❑ 1/4 C. old fashioned oats
- ❑ 1 (32 oz.) pkg. tater tots

Spices, Oils & Sauces:
- ❑ Salt and Pepper
- ❑ Hot pepper sauce
- ❑ 1 1/2 tsp. chicken bouillon
- ❑ 1 (32 oz.) jar spaghetti sauce
- ❑ Olive oil

Others:
- ❑ 3 1/2 T. sugar
- ❑ 1/2 C. brown sugar
- ❑ 1 tsp. baking powder
- ❑ 1 (10 3/4 oz.) can cream of celery soup
- ❑ 1 (10 3/4 oz.) can cream of mushroom soup
- ❑ 1 1/2 C. flour
- ❑ 4 T. lemon juice
- ❑ 1 C. slivered almonds
- ❑ 1 (16 oz.) can jellied cranberry sauce
- ❑ 1/2 C. real maple syrup

Breakfast
Day One:

Biscuits & Sausage Gravy

Makes 4 servings

1 (16 oz.) pkg. ground
   sausage
1 onion, chopped
3 T. flour
1 (12 oz.) can evaporated
   milk

1/2 C. water
1/8 tsp. salt
Hot pepper sauce to taste
1 tube of 8 refrigerated
   buttermilk biscuits

In a large skillet over medium high heat, cook ground sausage and chopped onions, stirring occasionally, until sausage is cooked throughout. Remove half of the cooked sausage and half of the onions to an airtight container.* Add flour, evaporated milk, water and salt to remaining sausage and onions in skillet. Cook, stirring occasionally, and add hot pepper sauce. Meanwhile, on a lightly greased baking sheet, cook refrigerated buttermilk biscuits according to package directions. Set aside 4 of the cooked biscuits.** To serve, split 1 baked buttermilk biscuit on each plate and spoon some of the sausage gravy mixture over biscuits.

*Reserve cooked sausage and onions for Breakfast on Day 2.
**Reserve 4 of the cooked biscuits for Dinner on Day 2.

Baked Chicken Salad

Makes 4 to 6 servings

8 boneless, skinless
   chicken breast halves
1 (10 3/4 oz.) can cream
   of celery soup
4 T. lemon juice
1 C. slivered almonds

1 C. mayonnaise
1 C. sour cream
1 C. shredded Cheddar
   cheese
2 C. crushed cornflakes

Preheat oven to 325°. In a large skillet over medium high heat, place chicken breast halves. Cook until chicken is cooked throughout and no longer pink. Remove chicken from skillet and chop or shred into pieces. Remove half of the cooked chopped chicken to an airtight container.* In an 8" or 9" square baking dish, combine remaining half of the chopped chicken, half of the cream of celery soup**, slivered almonds, mayonnaise, sour cream and shredded Cheddar cheese. Mix until well incorporated and sprinkle crushed cornflakes over mixture in baking dish. Bake in oven for 45 to 60 minutes, until heated throughout and cornflakes are lightly browned.

*Reserve half of the cooked chopped chicken for Dinner on Day 2.
**Reserve half of the cream of celery soup for Breakfast on Day 2.

Dinner
Day One:

Spaghetti with
Sweet & Sour Meatballs

Makes 4 to 6 servings

1 (14 oz.) can sauerkraut
1 (16 oz.) can jellied
   cranberry sauce
1/2 C. brown sugar

1 (32 oz.) jar spaghetti
   sauce
2 lbs. ground beef

Roll ground beef into desired size meatballs. In a medium saucepan over medium high heat, place meatballs. In a medium bowl, combine sauerkraut, cranberry sauce, brown sugar and half the jar of spaghetti sauce.* Pour sauerkraut mixture over meatballs in saucepan. Heat until meatballs are cooked throughout. Meanwhile, in a large pot of lightly salted water, cook spaghetti according to package directions, until al dente. Drain spaghetti and remove half of the cooked spaghetti to an airtight container.** To serve, divide remaining cooked spaghetti onto plates and spoon meatballs and some of the sauce over noodles on each plate.

*Reserve remaining spaghetti sauce for Dinner on Day 3.
**Reserve half of the cooked spaghetti for Lunch on Day 3.

Breakfast
Day Two:

Breakfast Pizza

Makes 4 to 6 servings

Leftover sausage and onions from Breakfast Day One
1 (10" to 12") prepared pizza crust
6 eggs
6 T. milk
Salt and pepper to taste

Leftover cream of celery soup from Lunch Day One
2 T. bacon bits
1 green bell pepper, minced
2 C. shredded Cheddar cheese

Preheat oven to 400°. Place pizza crust upside down on a baking sheet and bake in oven for 5 to 7 minutes, being careful not to burn. In a microwave-safe bowl, reheat leftover sausage and onion mixture from Day 1 in microwave. Remove mixture from microwave and drain of fat. In a separate bowl, whisk together eggs, milk, salt and pepper. In a medium skillet or pan over medium heat, scramble eggs until set. Remove crusts from oven, turn over and spread leftover cream of celery soup from Day 1 over crust. Spread egg mixture and heated sausage and onion mixture over crust. Sprinkle bacon bits and half of the minced green peppers* over sausage mixture on pizza crust. Top pizza with shredded Cheddar cheese and bake in oven for 25 to 30 minutes, until cheese is melted and crust is golden brown.
*Reserve remaining half of the minced green pepper for Dinner.

Tater-Baked Dish

Makes 4 to 6 servings

1 lb. ground beef	**1 (10 3/4 oz.) can cream**
Salt to taste	**of mushroom soup**
1 onion, chopped	**1/2 C. milk**
1 T. old fashioned oats	**1 (32 oz.) pkg. tater tots**

Preheat oven to 375°. Into a 9x13" baking dish, crumble ground beef. Add salt and chopped onion and mix by hand until thoroughly combined. Spread mixture evenly and sprinkle oats over top. In a small bowl, combine cream of mushroom soup and milk. Pour soup mixture over ground beef mixture in baking dish and top with tater tots. Bake in oven for 1 hour.

Dinner
Day Two:

Chicken á la RV

Makes 4 servings

1 (4 oz.) can sliced
    mushrooms, liquid
    reserved
Leftover minced green
    bell pepper from
    Breakfast
1/2 C. butter
1/2 C. flour
1 tsp. salt

1/4 tsp. pepper
1 1/2 tsp. chicken bouillon
1 1/2 C. milk
1 1/4 C. hot water
Leftover chopped chicken
    from Lunch Day One
Leftover cooked biscuits
    from Breakfast Day One

In a medium skillet or pan over medium heat, sauté sliced mushrooms and minced green peppers in butter. Cook until vegetables are softened, about 5 minutes and remove from heat. Stir in flour, salt and pepper. Return to low heat and cook until mixture is bubbly, stirring constantly. Remove from heat and stir in chicken bouillon, milk, water and reserved mushroom liquid. Return to heat and bring to a boil for 1 minute, stirring constantly. Stir in leftover chopped chicken from Day 1. Cook until mixture is heated throughout. To serve, set 1 split biscuit on each plate and spread additional butter over biscuits. Spoon a generous amount of the hot chicken mixture over biscuits on each plate.

Breakfast
Day Three:

Maple Flavored Muffins

Makes 6 muffins

3/4 C. flour
2 T. sugar
1 tsp. baking powder
1/4 tsp. salt
2 T. butter

2 T. old fashioned oats
1 egg, beaten
1/2 C. milk
1/2 C. real maple syrup

Preheat oven to 400°. Grease 6 muffin cups and set aside. Into a medium bowl, sift flour, sugar, baking powder and salt. Using a pastry blender, cut in butter until mixture resembles coarse crumbs. Stir in oats, eggs, milk and syrup. Stir just until moistened and fill each muffin cup 3/4 full of batter. Bake in oven for 18 to 20 minutes. Remove muffins from oven and let cool slightly before removing from muffin cups.

*Start preparing manicotti for Dinner (see page 40).

Lunch
Day Three:

Broccoli Noodle Soup

Makes 4 servings

6 C. water
1 head broccoli, chopped
Pinch of salt
Leftover cooked spaghetti
    from Dinner Day One

1/4 C. olive oil
Pepper to taste
1 small loaf crusty bread,
    cut into thick slices

Place water in a large pot over medium heat. Stir in chopped broccoli and salt, heating until broccoli is tender. Chop leftover spaghetti noodles from Day 1 into smaller pieces. Continue to cook and add chopped spaghetti noodles to soup. Spoon soup into bowl and top each serving with 1 tablespoon olive oil and pepper. Serve with thick slices of crusty bread.

Dinner
Day Three:

Spinach Manicotti

Makes 4 to 6 servings

2 C. ricotta cheese
2 eggs
1 (10 oz.) pkg. frozen
  chopped spinach,
  thawed and drained
1 C. shredded mozzarella
  cheese
1/2 C. grated Parmesan
  cheese, divided

1 1/2 T. sugar
1/8 tsp. salt
1/4 tsp. pepper
10 to 12 large manicotti
  shells
Leftover spaghetti sauce
  from Dinner Day One

In a medium bowl, combine ricotta cheese and eggs, mixing until blended. Stir in drained spinach, shredded mozzarella cheese, 1/4 cup grated Parmesan cheese, sugar, salt and pepper. Mix well and stuff mixture into the manicotti shells. Spread half of the leftover spaghetti sauce from Day 1 evenly into the bottom of a 9x13" baking dish. Arrange stuffed manicotti shells in a single layer over sauce in pan. Pour remaining sauce over shells, cover dish tightly with aluminum foil and chill in refrigerator for 6 to 8 hours. Preheat oven to 400°. Bake chilled manicotti in oven for 40 minutes. Sprinkle remaining 1/4 cup grated Parmesan cheese over noodles and return to oven, uncovered, for an additional 15 minutes.

40

Trip Five

SHOPPING LIST

Dairy & Eggs:
- ❑ 12 large eggs
- ❑ 3 sticks butter
- ❑ 1 T. heavy cream
- ❑ 2 C. sour cream
- ❑ 1 small can grated Parmesan cheese
- ❑ 3 1/2 C. shredded Cheddar cheese
- ❑ 1 1/4 C. milk
- ❑ 1 (5 oz.) can evaporated milk

Fruits & Vegetables:
- ❑ 2 onions
- ❑ 1 red bell pepper
- ❑ 2 stalks celery
- ❑ 2 lbs. fresh asparagus spears
- ❑ 1 C. chopped broccoli
- ❑ 2 medium potatoes
- ❑ 6 green onions
- ❑ 1 large cucumber
- ❑ 4 small heads butter lettuce
- ❑ 1 (8 oz.) can pineapple chunks

Meats:
- ❑ 12 large slices Canadian bacon
- ❑ 1 boneless, skinless chicken breast
- ❑ 8 slices bacon
- ❑ 1 (6 oz.) can tuna

Spices, Oils & Sauces:
- ❑ Salt and Pepper
- ❑ White wine vinegar
- ❑ Cayenne pepper
- ❑ Dried oregano
- ❑ Dry mustard
- ❑ 1 small bottle vegetable oil
- ❑ Chili powder
- ❑ Worcestershire sauce
- ❑ Garlic powder
- ❑ 2 T. Dijon mustard
- ❑ Dried dillweed

Breads & Grains:
- ❑ 4 English muffins, split
- ❑ 12 slices white or wheat bread
- ❑ 1 (12 oz.) pkg. medium egg noodles
- ❑ 1 C. long-grain white rice
- ❑ 1 (14 oz.) tube refrigerated pizza crust dough

Others:
- ❑ 1 T. lemon juice
- ❑ 1 (26 oz.) can tomato soup
- ❑ 2 C. chicken broth
- ❑ 1 C. flour
- ❑ 1 3/4 T. sugar
- ❑ 1 tsp. baking powder
- ❑ 1 C. pizza sauce

Breakfast
Day One:

Easy Eggs Benedict

Makes 4 servings

12 large slices Canadian
    bacon
1 tsp. white wine vinegar
5 eggs
1 T. heavy cream

Dash of cayenne pepper
1/2 tsp. salt
1 T. lemon juice
4 English muffins, split

In a medium skillet over medium high heat, fry the Canadian bacon on both sides until evenly browned. Remove cooked Canadian bacon from skillet and wrap all but 4 of the slices of Canadian bacon and place in refrigerator.* In a large saucepan over medium heat, place 3" of water. Add vinegar and bring to a simmer. Carefully break 4 eggs into simmering water and cook for 2 to 3 minutes, until whites of eggs are set but yolks are still soft. Remove eggs from saucepan with a slotted spoon. Meanwhile, in a microwave-safe bowl, place butter. Heat butter in microwave until melted. In a separate bowl, using a whisk, thoroughly blend egg yolk of remaining 1 egg, heavy cream, cayenne pepper and salt. Slowly pour in melted butter, whisking constantly. Slowly add lemon juice and remaining melted butter, whisking constantly and thoroughly. Toast English muffins halves and place two English muffin halves on each plate. Place 1 slice of the remaining cooked Canadian bacon on 1 of the English muffins on each plate. Top with 1 poached egg and drizzle butter mixture over egg. Serve immediately.

*Reserve 8 cooked Canadian bacon slices for Lunch on Day 2 and Dinner on Day 3.

Lunch
Day One:

Grilled Cheese &
Tomato Soup

Makes 4 servings

1 (26 oz.) can tomato soup
8 slices white or wheat
   bread

Butter
1 C. shredded Cheddar
   cheese, divided

In a large soup pot over medium heat, place half the can of tomato soup.* Cook soup according to package directions by adding milk or water as needed. Meanwhile, spread butter over both sides of each slice of bread. Place four slices of buttered bread in heated skillet. Sprinkle 1/4 cup shredded Cheddar cheese over each slice of bread and top with another slice of buttered bread. Heat until bread is lightly browned on one side and flip each sandwich over. Cook sandwiches until other side is lightly browned and cheese is melted. To serve, ladle soup into four bowls and serve with grilled cheese sandwiches.
*Reserve remaining half of the tomato soup for Dinner on Day 3.

Dinner
Day One:

Asparagus Chicken Bake

Makes 6 servings

1 (12 oz.) pkg. medium
  egg noodles
1 1/3 T. vegetable oil
1 onion, chopped
1 boneless, skinless
  chicken breast
1 red bell pepper, chopped
2 stalks celery, chopped

1 C. chicken broth
1 1/2 C. sour cream
1/2 tsp. dried oregano
2 lbs. fresh asparagus
  spears
1/2 C. grated Parmesan
  cheese

Preheat oven to 350°. In a large pot of lightly salted water, cook egg noodles according to package directions, about 6 to 8 minutes, until al dente. Rinse pasta under cool water and remove half of the cooked pasta to an airtight container.* Fill a separate large pot with lightly salted water and bring to a boil. Cook asparagus in boiling water until tender, about 1 to 2 minutes. Remove half of the cooked asparagus and place in an airtight container.** Rinse remaining asparagus under cool running water. In a large skillet over medium heat, place vegetable oil. Add chopped onions and sauté until onions are tender, about 4 to 5 minutes. Add chicken breast and heat until cooked throughout. Remove cooked chicken breast to a plate and chop or shred into pieces. Return chopped chicken to skillet and add chopped red bell pepper, chopped celery and chicken broth. Bring to a boil, reduce heat and let simmer for 5 minutes. Stir in sour cream and oregano. Spread half of the chicken mixture in a 9x13" baking dish. Arrange remaining cooked asparagus and remaining cooked noodles over chicken mixture. Top with remaining chicken mixture and sprinkle with grated Parmesan cheese. Bake in oven for 30 minutes, until lightly browned.

*Reserve half of the cooked pasta for Dinner on Day 2.
**Reserve half of the cooked asparagus for Lunch on Day 3.

Breakfast
Day Two:

Breakfast Casserole

Makes 4 to 6 servings

8 slices bacon
1 C. chopped broccoli
4 slices white or wheat
    bread
1 T. butter, softened
1/2 C. shredded Cheddar
    cheese

6 eggs
1 C. milk
1/4 tsp. dry mustard
Salt and pepper to taste

Preheat oven to 325°. In a large skillet over medium high heat, place bacon. Cook bacon until browned and remove to paper towels to drain. Crumble bacon and set aside half of the crumbled bacon.* In a medium pot of boiling water, cook chopped broccoli until tender but firm, about 10 minutes. Drain broccoli and set aside. Lightly grease an 8" square baking dish. Spread butter over each slice of bread and line the bottom of the pan with the buttered bread. Cover bread with shredded Cheddar cheese, remaining half of the crumbled bacon and cooked broccoli. In a large bowl, using a whisk, combine eggs, milk, dry mustard, salt and pepper. Mix well and pour over ingredients in pan. Bake in oven for 20 minutes, until eggs are completely cooked, about 1 hour.

*Reserve half of the cooked crumbled bacon for Breakfast on Day 3.

Lunch
Day Two:

Potato Bacon Soup

Makes 4 to 6 servings

2 T. butter
1 onion, chopped
2 medium potatoes,
    peeled and quartered
1 C. chicken broth
1 (5 oz.) can evaporated
    milk

Leftover cooked Canadian
    bacon from Breakfast
    Day One
1/4 tsp. salt
1/8 tsp. pepper
4 T. sour cream
2 green onions, chopped

In a large soup pot over medium heat, place butter. Heat until butter is melted and add chopped onions. Sauté onions until softened and add quartered potatoes and chicken broth. Bring to a boil, reduce heat and let simmer for 20 to 25 minutes until potatoes are tender. In a blender or food processor, puree heated mixture in batches and return to soup pot. Chop the leftover Canadian bacon from Day 1. Stir in evaporated milk, half of the chopped Canadian bacon*, salt and pepper. Return to medium heat and cook until heated throughout, being careful not to boil. Ladle soup into bowls and garnish each serving with 1 tablespoon sour cream and some of the chopped green onions.

*Reserve remaining chopped Canadian bacon for Dinner on Day 3.

Dinner
Day Two:

Tuna Noodle Casserole

Makes 4 servings

**Leftover cooked noodles
    from Dinner Day One**
1 T. vegetable oil
**Leftover tomato soup
    from Lunch Day One**
1 tsp. chili powder

1/2 tsp. salt
1 tsp. Worcestershire sauce
**1 1/4 C. shredded Cheddar
    cheese**
1 (6 oz.) can tuna, drained

Preheat oven to 350°. In a large skillet over medium heat, place vegetable oil. Add chopped onions and sauté until tender. Add remaining undiluted tomato soup from Day 1, chili powder, salt and Worcestershire sauce. Bring to a simmer and mix in cooked noodles from Day 1, 1 cup shredded Cheddar cheese and drained tuna. Mix well and transfer mixture to a greased 9" square baking dish. Bake in oven for 30 minutes. Remove from oven and immediately sprinkle remaining 1/4 cup shredded Cheddar cheese over hot casserole.

Breakfast
Day Three:

Bacon Cheddar Muffins

Makes 6 muffins

**Leftover crumbled bacon
    from Breakfast Day Two**
1 C. flour
3/4 T. sugar
1 tsp. baking powder
1/8 tsp. salt
3/4 tsp. garlic powder
1 green onion, chopped

**2 1/2 T. grated Parmesan
    cheese**
**1/2 C. shredded Cheddar
    cheese**
1 egg, beaten
1/4 C. milk
1/4 C. vegetable oil

Preheat oven to 400°. Lightly grease 6 muffin cups and set aside. In a large bowl, combine flour, sugar, baking powder, salt, garlic powder, chopped green onion, grated Parmesan cheese, shredded Cheddar cheese and leftover crumbled bacon from Day 2. In a separate bowl, using a whisk, combine egg, milk and vegetable oil. Mix well and stir mixture into dry ingredients, mixing just until moistened. Spoon batter into prepared muffin cups. Bake in oven for 20 minutes, or until a toothpick inserted in center of muffins comes out clean.

Lunch
Day Three:

Cucumber Asparagus Salad

Makes 4 to 6 servings

1 3/4 C. water	2 T. Dijon mustard
1 C. long-grain white rice	1 T. sugar
Leftover cooked asparagus	1 T. white wine vinegar
from Dinner Day One	1/2 tsp. dry mustard
1 large cucumber, peeled,	2 1/2 T. vegetable oil
seeded and chopped	1 tsp. dried dillweed
3 green onions, chopped	4 small heads butter lettuce

In a medium saucepan over medium heat, bring water to a boil. Add rice, return to a boil, reduce heat, cover and let cook until water is absorbed and rice is tender, about 20 minutes. Fluff rice with a fork, remove from heat and let cool to room temperature. Cut leftover cooked asparagus into 1" pieces. Add asparagus pieces, chopped cucumber and chopped green onions to rice. In a medium bowl, whisk together Dijon mustard, sugar, white wine vinegar, dry mustard, vegetable oil and dried dillweed. Pour dressing over rice ingredients and toss until well incorporated. Fill a large serving bowl with torn lettuce and top with rice and asparagus mixture.

Dinner
Day Three:

Hawaiian Pizza

Makes 4 to 6 servings

1 (14 oz.) tube refrigerated pizza crust dough
Leftover chopped Canadian bacon from Lunch Day Two

1 (8 oz.) can pineapple chunks, drained
1 C. pizza sauce

Preheat oven to 350°. Press refrigerated pizza crust dough evenly onto a lightly greased 10" to 12" pizza pan. Spread pizza sauce over pizza crust to within 1/2" from the edge. Sprinkle cooked chopped Canadian bacon from Lunch on Day 2 over pizza sauce and spread pineapple chunks over Canadian bacon. Sprinkle shredded mozzarella cheese over pizza and bake in oven for 15 to 20 minutes, or until crust is lightly browned and cheese is melted.

Trip Six

SHOPPING LIST

Dairy & Eggs:
- ☐ 9 eggs
- ☐ 2 C. milk
- ☐ 5 sticks butter
- ☐ 1/4 C. grated Parmesan cheese
- ☐ 1/4 C. shredded Monterey Jack cheese
- ☐ 1 C. American cheese
- ☐ 3 C. shredded Cheddar cheese

Fruits & Vegetables:
- ☐ 1 (24 oz.) jar medium salsa
- ☐ 2 onions
- ☐ 1 green bell pepper
- ☐ 2 cloves garlic
- ☐ 1 (14 1/2 oz.) can diced tomatoes with jalapenos
- ☐ 1 (4 oz.) can diced green chilies
- ☐ 2 1/2 C. golden raisins
- ☐ 1 small head lettuce
- ☐ 1 C. prepared coleslaw
- ☐ 4 green onions
- ☐ 1 (4 oz.) can sliced mushrooms

Meats:
- ☐ 3 1/2 lbs. ground beef

Breads & Grains:
- ☐ 8 slices thick-cut bread
- ☐ 8 slices multi-grain bread
- ☐ 1 C. crushed saltine crackers
- ☐ 1 (32 oz.) box uncooked macaroni
- ☐ 5 C. uncooked brown rice
- ☐ 8 (8") flour tortillas
- ☐ 4 C. whole bran cereal

Spices, Oils & Sauces:
- ☐ Salt and Pepper
- ☐ Almond extract
- ☐ Vanilla
- ☐ 1 small bottle vegetable oil
- ☐ Cinnamon
- ☐ Ground cardamom
- ☐ 4 T. Dijon mustard

Others:
- ☐ 2 1/2 C. slivered almonds
- ☐ 2 1/2 C. flour
- ☐ 1/2 tsp. baking powder
- ☐ 2 tsp. baking soda
- ☐ Powdered sugar
- ☐ 2 (29 oz.) cans tomato sauce
- ☐ 1/4 C. maple syrup
- ☐ 1 (1 1/4 oz.) env. taco seasoning
- ☐ 2 C. pineapple juice
- ☐ 1 C. brown sugar
- ☐ 1/2 C. honey
- ☐ 2 (10 3/4 oz.) cans cream of mushroom soup

Breakfast
Day One:

Almond French Toast

Makes 4 servings

2 1/2 C. slivered almonds
3 eggs
1 C. milk
3 T. flour
1/4 tsp. salt
1/2 tsp. baking powder

1/2 tsp. almond extract
1 tsp. vanilla
8 slices thick-cut bread
3 T. vegetable oil
3 T. butter
Powdered sugar for dusting

In a small saucepan over low heat, place slivered almonds. Toast almonds until lightly browned, about 5 to 10 minutes, tossing frequently. Set aside 1 1/2 cups of the toasted slivered almonds.* In a large bowl, using a whisk, combine eggs, milk, flour, salt, baking powder, almond extract and vanilla. Mix well and soak each slice of bread in milk mixture until saturated. Place soaked slices of bread in a shallow pan and chill in refrigerator at least 30 minutes. Meanwhile, in a large skillet over medium heat, place vegetable oil. Place toasted slivered almonds in a shallow dish. Press slices of bread, one at a time, in the toasted almonds, until coated. Fry coated bread slices in skillet until golden brown on each side. Remove French toast to a plate and dust with powdered sugar.
*Reserve 1 1/2 cups toasted slivered almonds for Breakfast on Day 2 and Dinner on Day 3.

Lunch
Day One:

Monterey Meatloaf

Makes 4 to 6 servings

1 lb. ground beef
1 1/2 C. medium salsa
1/4 C. grated Parmesan
  cheese

1/4 C. shredded Monterey
  Jack cheese
1 egg
1 C. crushed saltine crackers

Preheat oven to 350°. Grease a 5x9" loaf pan and set aside. In a large bowl, combine ground beef, salsa, grated Parmesan cheese, shredded Monterey Jack cheese, egg and crushed saltine crackers. Mix by hand until well combined and shape mixture into a loaf. Place loaf in prepared pan and bake in oven for 1 hour, or until internal temperature of meatloaf registers at 160° on a meat thermometer. Meatloaf is done when browned throughout and juices run clear. Remove from oven and cut loaf in half. Wrap and set aside half of the cooked meatloaf.* Cut remaining half of the meatloaf into slices and serve.

*Reserve half of the cooked meatloaf for Lunch on Day 3.

Dinner
Day One:

Macaroni Casserole

Makes 4 servings

1 (32 oz.) box uncooked
    macaroni
1 1/2 lbs. ground beef
1 onion, chopped

1 green bell pepper,
    chopped
2 (29 oz.) cans tomato
    sauce

In a large pot of lightly salted water, cook macaroni according to package directions, until al dente. Drain pasta and transfer half of the cooked pasta to an airtight container.* In a large skillet over medium heat, place ground beef. Cook ground beef until cooked throughout. Add chopped onions and sauté until onions are softened. Add chopped green bell pepper and tomato sauce. Continue to cook until heated throughout and green peppers are softened. To serve, place remaining cooked pasta evenly on four serving plates. Spoon a generous amount of the ground beef mixture over pasta and serve.
*Reserve half of the cooked macaroni pasta for Lunch on Day 2.

Breakfast
Day Two:

Rice & Raisin
Breakfast Pudding

Makes 4 servings

1 C. water	Leftover toasted slivered
1 C. uncooked brown rice	almonds from Breakfast
1/2 C. golden raisins	Day One
1/4 C. maple syrup	1 tsp. cinnamon
1 C. milk	1/2 tsp. ground cardamom

In a medium saucepan over medium high heat, bring water to a boil. Add brown rice, reduce heat, cover and let simmer for 45 minutes, stirring occasionally, until rice is tender and has absorbed most of the water. After rice has cooked, add golden raisins, maple syrup, milk, 1/2 cup of the leftover toasted almonds from Day 1*, cinnamon and ground cardamom. Bring mixture to a boil and immediately reduce heat to a simmer. Let simmer for about 5 to 8 minutes, stirring frequently, until mixture is thickened. To serve, spoon mixture into bowls.

*Reserve remaining 1 cup toasted slivered almonds for Dinner on Day 3.

Lunch
Day Two:

Microwave Mac & Cheese

Makes 4 to 6 servings

Leftover cooked macaroni pasta from Dinner Day One
1/2 C. butter

1 C. American cheese
1/2 C. shredded Cheddar cheese

Place leftover cooked macaroni from Day 1 in a medium bowl. Cut butter and American cheese into pieces. Place butter pieces, American cheese pieces and shredded Cheddar cheese in a bowl. Microwave for 1 minute, remove from microwave and stir well. Return to microwave for 1 additional minute, or until mixture is completely melted. Stir vigorously and immediately pour melted cheese sauce over cooked macaroni pasta in bowl. Toss until fully coated and serve immediately.

Dinner
Day Two:

Baja Beef Tacos

Makes 4 servings

2 T. vegetable oil
1 onion, chopped
2 cloves garlic, minced
1 lb. ground beef
1 (14 1/2 oz.) can diced
    tomatoes with jalapenos
1 (4 oz.) can diced green
    chilies, drained

1 (1 1/4 oz.) env. taco
    seasoning
Medium salsa
8 (8") flour tortillas
1 small head lettuce,
    shredded
1 C. shredded Cheddar
    cheese

In a medium skillet over medium heat, place vegetable oil. Sauté chopped onions and minced garlic in oil for 3 minutes. Add ground beef and cook, stirring occasionally, until browned throughout, about 6 minutes. Stir in diced tomatoes with jalapenos, drained green chilies and taco seasoning. Bring mixture to a boil, reduce heat and let simmer for 5 minutes. To assemble tacos, place 1/2 cup of the meat mixture in the center of each flour tortilla. Top with some of the medium salsa, shredded lettuce and shredded Cheddar cheese. Place two tacos on each of four serving plates and serve.
*Prepare batter for muffins for Breakfast on Day 3.

Honey Bran Muffins

Makes 10 muffins

2 C. pineapple juice	**4 C. whole bran cereal**
2 C. golden raisins	**1 C. brown sugar**
2 C. flour	**1/2 C. vegetable oil**
2 tsp. baking soda	**1/2 C. honey**
1 tsp. salt	**5 eggs, beaten**

In a small bowl, combine pineapple juice and golden raisins. Mix lightly and set aside. In a medium bowl, combine flour, baking soda and salt. Mix well and stir in whole bran cereal and set aside. In a large bowl, combine brown sugar, vegetable oil, honey and beaten eggs. Mix well and stir in bran cereal mixture. Stir until well combined and fold in pineapple juice and raisins. Mix well. The batter will be thin. Cover and chill batter in refrigerator overnight. In morning, lightly grease 10 muffin cups and stir the chilled batter. Fill each muffin cup 3/4 full with batter. Bake in oven for 20 to 25 minutes, or until a toothpick inserted in center of muffins comes out clean. Remove muffins from oven and let cool on a wire rack for 10 minutes before removing from cups.

Lunch
Day Three:

Sweet & Sour Meatloaf Sandwiches

Makes 4 servings

1 C. prepared coleslaw
8 slices multi-grain bread
4 T. Dijon mustard

Leftover cooked meatloaf
from Dinner Day One

Reheat cooked meatloaf from Day 1 in the microwave. Spread 1 tablespoon Dijon mustard over 4 slices of multi-grain bread. Place 1/4 cup prepared coleslaw over Dijon mustard on 4 slices of bread. Cut leftover cooked meatloaf into 4 thick slices and place 1 slice over coleslaw. Top each slice of meatloaf with an additional slice of multi-grain bread to make 4 sandwiches. If desired, the bread may be toasted before assembling the sandwiches.

Dinner
Day Three:

Baked Almond Rice Casserole

Makes 4 to 6 servings

8 C. water
4 C. uncooked brown rice
1/2 C. butter
4 green onions, chopped
2 (10 3/4 oz.) cans cream of mushroom soup
1 (4 oz.) can sliced mushrooms, drained

Leftover toasted slivered almonds from Breakfast Day Two
1 1/2 C. shredded Cheddar cheese

Preheat oven to 350°. In a large saucepan over medium high heat, bring water to a boil. Add rice, reduce heat, cover and let simmer for 20 minutes, stirring occasionally. Meanwhile, in a small saucepan over medium heat, place butter. When butter has melted, stir in chopped green onions and sauté until onions are softened. Stir in cream of mushroom soup, cooked brown rice, drained mushrooms and remaining 1 cup toasted slivered almonds from Day 2. Spoon half of the mixture into 1 1/2" quart baking dish. Sprinkle half of the shredded Cheddar cheese over the mixture and top with remaining half of the rice mixture. Sprinkle remaining half of the shredded Cheddar cheese over rice mixture and bake in oven for 20 minutes, or until casserole is heated throughout and cheese is melted.

Trip Seven

SHOPPING LIST

Dairy & Eggs:
- ❑ 16 eggs
- ❑ 1 stick butter
- ❑ 3 1/2 C. shredded Monterey Jack cheese
- ❑ 1/2 C. sour cream
- ❑ 1/2 C. cream cheese
- ❑ 1 C. milk
- ❑ 1 C. crumbled blue cheese
- ❑ 4 C. shredded Cheddar cheese
- ❑ 1 (6 oz.) container plain yogurt
- ❑ 1/2 C. mayonnaise

Fruits & Vegetables:
- ❑ 5 large avocados
- ❑ 1 (24 oz.) jar medium salsa
- ❑ 1 (16 oz.) can refried beans
- ❑ 3 cloves garlic
- ❑ 7 small tomatoes
- ❑ 3 green onions
- ❑ 2 small onions
- ❑ 1 green bell pepper
- ❑ 1 jalapeno pepper
- ❑ 1 large head lettuce, shredded or torn
- ❑ 1 (8 oz.) pkg. sliced fresh mushrooms

Meats:
- ❑ 8 slices bacon
- ❑ 2 1/2 lbs. ground beef
- ❑ 6 (8 oz.) New York strip steaks
- ❑ 1 (2 lb.) bag frozen cooked shrimp

Breads & Grains:
- ❑ 4 bagels
- ❑ 6 hamburger buns
- ❑ 4 (6") corn tortillas
- ❑ 3/4 C. long-grain white rice
- ❑ 6 (10") flour tortillas

Spices, Oils & Sauces:
- ❑ Salt and pepper
- ❑ 1 1/2 C. steak sauce
- ❑ Dried dillweed
- ❑ Worcestershire sauce
- ❑ Dried minced onion
- ❑ Hot pepper sauce
- ❑ Dry mustard
- ❑ 1 small bottle vegetable oil
- ❑ 3 T. red wine vinegar
- ❑ 1/8 tsp. liquid smoke flavoring
- ❑ Cumin
- ❑ Garlic salt

Others:
- ❑ 1 (1 1/4 oz.) env. taco seasoning
- ❑ 1 small bottle lemon juice
- ❑ 2 (10 1/2 oz.) cans chicken broth
- ❑ 1/4 C. walnuts

Breakfast
Day One:

Bacon & Avocado Omelet

Makes 4 to 6 servings

8 slices bacon	1 large avocado, peeled
8 eggs	and cut into 1/2" pieces
6 T. water	1 1/2 C. shredded Monterey
Salt and pepper to taste	Jack cheese
3 T. butter	2 1/2 C. medium salsa

In a medium skillet over medium high heat, cook bacon until browned and remove to paper towels to drain. Crumble the bacon and set aside. Drain skillet of fat. In a medium bowl, whisk together eggs, water, salt and pepper. In the same skillet over medium high heat, place butter. When butter has melted, swirl skillet until coated. Pour 1/4 of the egg mixture into skillet. Heat for about 2 minutes, until egg mixture begins to set at the bottom of the pan. Gently lift edges of egg and push inward so the uncooked part of the egg mixture flows toward the edges. Continue to cook until the center of the omelet starts to look dry, about 2 to 3 minutes. Sprinkle some of the crumbled bacon, avocado pieces and shredded Monterey Jack cheese over half of the omelet. Cook for 1 minute, until cheese begins to melt. Fold omelet over the filling and slide onto a plate. Repeat with remaining egg mixture, bacon, avocado and shredded cheese. Serve omelets with salsa.

Taco Bake

Makes 4 servings

1 lb. ground beef
1 (1 1/4 oz.) env. taco
  seasoning
1 (16 oz.) can refried beans

2 C. medium salsa
2 C. shredded Monterey
  Jack cheese

Preheat oven to 325°. In a large skillet over medium high heat, brown ground beef until cooked throughout and drain skillet of fat. Stir in taco seasoning and mix well. Transfer mixture to a 9" square baking dish. Spread half the can of refried beans over meat mixture in baking dish.* Top with salsa and shredded Monterey Jack cheese. Bake in oven for 20 to 25 minutes, until heated throughout and cheese is melted.

*Reserve remaining half can of refried beans for Dinner on Day 3.

Dinner
Day One:

Grilled Steaks with Guacamole Salad

Makes 4 servings

6 (8 oz.) New York strip
   steaks
1 1/2 C. steak sauce
1 tsp. pepper
2 large avocados, peeled
1/4 C. lemon juice

1/2 C. sour cream
1 clove garlic, pressed
2 tsp. dried dillweed
1 tsp. Worcestershire sauce
1 small tomato, chopped

In a large ziplock bag, place strip steaks, steak sauce and pepper. Place bag with steaks and marinade in refrigerator and chill for 30 minutes. Meanwhile, in a medium bowl, mash 1 avocado. Stir in lemon juice, sour cream, minced garlic, dried dillweed, Worcestershire sauce and chopped tomato. Chop remaining avocado into pieces. Stir in pieces of avocado, cover and chill guacamole salad until steaks are done. Preheat grill or place a large skillet over medium high heat. Remove steaks from refrigerator and discard the marinade. Grill steaks or cook in skillet for 5 to 7 minutes on each side, or to desired doneness. Remove 2 of the cooked steaks, wrap and place in refrigerator.* Place 1 steak on each of four serving plates and serve with chilled guacamole salad on the side.

*Reserve two cooked steaks for Lunch on Day 3.

Breakfast
Day Two:

Tomato Breakfast Bagels

Makes 4 servings

1/2 C. cream cheese
1/2 T. dried dillweed
4 bagels, split

1 small tomato, sliced
Salt and pepper to taste

In a medium bowl, combine cream cheese and dried dillweed, mixing until well incorporated. Toast each bagel and place two bagel halves on each of four serving plates. Spread 2 tablespoons of the cream cheese mixture over one bagel half on each plate. Top bagel halves with some of the tomato slices and sprinkle with salt and pepper. Top with remaining toasted bagel half to make four sandwiches.

Lunch
Day Two:

Avocado Shrimp Bisque

Makes 4 to 6 servings

1 (2 lb.) bag frozen
   cooked shrimp
2 large avocados, peeled
   and chopped
1 (10 1/2 oz.) can chicken
   broth

1 C. milk
1/2 tsp. lemon juice
1 tsp. dried minced onion
Salt and pepper to taste

    Thaw the frozen cooked shrimp and chop into small pieces, discarding the tails. Set aside half of the chopped shrimp.* In a medium saucepan over medium heat, combine chopped avocados, chicken broth, milk, lemon juice and dried minced onion. Slowly bring mixture to a boil, stirring frequently. Reduce heat and add remaining chopped cooked shrimp, salt and pepper. Mix well and cook until heated throughout, being careful not to boil. Remove from heat and, if desired, add more salt and pepper to taste. To serve, spoon bisque into bowls. Can be served hot or cold.

*Reserve half of the chopped shrimp for Dinner on Day 3.

Dinner
Day Two:

Blue Cheese Burgers

Makes 6 burgers

1 1/2 lbs. ground beef
1/4 C. crumbled blue cheese
3 green onions, chopped
1/8 tsp. hot pepper sauce

1/2 tsp. Worcestershire sauce
Salt and pepper to taste
1/2 tsp. dry mustard
6 hamburger buns

Preheat grill or place a large skillet over high heat. In a large bowl, combine ground beef, crumbled blue cheese, chopped green onion, hot pepper sauce, Worcestershire sauce, salt, pepper and dry mustard. Mix by hand until well incorporated and shape mixture into 6 hamburger patties. Lightly oil the grate or spray skillet with non-stick cooking spray. Place burgers on hot grill or in hot skillet and cook for 5 minutes per side, until cooked to desired doneness. Serve on hamburger buns.

Breakfast
Day Three:

Eggs Rancho Huevos

Makes 4 servings

8 eggs
1 small tomato, diced
1 small onion, chopped
1 green bell pepper,
  chopped
1 jalapeno pepper,
  seeded and diced

4 T. butter
4 (6") corn tortillas, cut
  into strips
1 C. shredded Cheddar
  cheese

In a large bowl, lightly beat eggs. Stir in diced tomato, chopped onion, chopped green bell pepper and diced jalapeno pepper. In a large skillet over medium heat, place butter. Heat until butter is melted and add corn tortilla strips. Toss corn tortilla strips until slightly softened. Add egg mixture and stir until well combined. Cook, stirring occasionally, until eggs are set. Sprinkle shredded Cheddar cheese over egg mixture and continue to heat until cheese is melted. To serve, spoon some of the egg mixture onto each plate.

Lunch
Day Three:

Steak Salad

Makes 4 servings

**Reserve cooked steak
   from Dinner Day One**
**1 large head lettuce,
   shredded or torn**
3 small tomatoes, sliced
**1 (8 oz.) pkg. sliced fresh
   mushrooms**
3/4 C. crumbled blue cheese
1/4 C. walnuts

1/3 C. vegetable oil
3 T. red wine vinegar
2 T. lemon juice
1/2 tsp. salt
1/8 tsp. pepper
3 tsp. Worcestershire sauce
**1/8 tsp. liquid smoke
   flavoring**

Slice leftover cooked steaks from Day 1 into bite-size pieces. In a large bowl, combine shredded lettuce, sliced tomatoes, sliced mushrooms, crumbled blue cheese, walnuts and sliced steak. In a small bowl, whisk together vegetable oil, red wine vinegar, lemon juice, salt, pepper, Worcestershire sauce and liquid smoke flavoring. Mix until well combined and pour dressing over ingredients in bowl. Toss until evenly coated.

Shrimp Burritos

Makes 6 burritos

2 T. vegetable oil
1 small onion, chopped
3/4 C. long-grain white
    rice
3/4 tsp. cumin
1 1/2 tsp. garlic salt,
    divided
1 (10 1/2 oz.) can chicken
    broth
1 small tomato, diced
Leftover refried beans
    from Lunch Day One

1/2 tsp. pepper
Leftover cooked shrimp
    from Lunch Day Two
2 cloves garlic, minced
1 (6 oz.) container plain
    yogurt
1/2 C. mayonnaise
6 (10") flour tortillas
3 C. shredded Cheddar
cheese
Medium salsa

In a medium saucepan over medium heat, place vegetable oil. Add chopped onions and sauté until softened. Stir in rice, cumin and 3/4 teaspoon garlic salt. Stir until rice is lightly toasted, about 5 minutes. Add chicken broth and diced tomatoes. Bring mixture to a boil, reduce heat, cover and let simmer for 15 to 20 minutes, until all liquid has been absorbed. In a small saucepan over medium heat, combine leftover refried beans from Day 1, remaining 3/4 teaspoon garlic salt and pepper. Cook until heated throughout and remove from heat. In a medium skillet over medium heat, place leftover cooked shrimp from Day 2 and minced garlic. Sauté shrimp until heated throughout, stirring occasionally. In a small bowl, whisk together yogurt and mayonnaise. To assemble burritos, place an even amount of the heated beans mixture over each tortilla. Top with about 1/2 cup of the shrimp mixture, about 1/4 cup of the rice mixture and some of the shredded Cheddar cheese. Add medium salsa to taste, roll up burritos to enclose filling and serve.

Trip Eight

SHOPPING LIST

Dairy & Eggs:
- ☐ 2 C. shredded Cheddar cheese
- ☐ 18 eggs
- ☐ 2 1/4 C. milk
- ☐ 1/4 C. plus 1 T. butter
- ☐ 2 C. shredded mozzarella cheese
- ☐ 3 T. grated Parmesan cheese
- ☐ 1 (8 oz.) pkg. cream cheese

Fruits & Vegetables:
- ☐ 2 heads Napa cabbage (1 small, 1 large)
- ☐ 6 green onions
- ☐ 2 1/2 lbs. russet potatoes
- ☐ 4 green onions
- ☐ 3 onions (1 small, 2 medium)
- ☐ 1 red bell pepper
- ☐ 2 cloves garlic
- ☐ 1 jalapeno pepper
- ☐ 4 (15 oz.) cans black beans
- ☐ 1 (20 oz.) can crushed pineapple in juice
- ☐ 1 tomato

Meats:
- ☐ 12 slices bacon
- ☐ 1 (10 lb.) bone-in ham
- ☐ 3 (6 oz.) cans chunk light tuna

Breads & Grains:
- ☐ 1 (11 oz.) pkg. pie crust mix
- ☐ 1 (3 oz.) pkg. chicken flavored ramen noodles
- ☐ 4 (10") flour tortillas

Spices, Oils & Sauces:
- ☐ Salt and Pepper
- ☐ Nutmeg
- ☐ 1 small bottle vegetable oil
- ☐ 1/4 C. rice wine vinegar
- ☐ 1 T. soy sauce
- ☐ 1 T. sesame oil
- ☐ 1/4 C. whole cloves
- ☐ 4 T. fresh chopped cilantro
- ☐ Paprika

Others:
- ☐ 1/2 C. sesame seeds
- ☐ 1/2 C. slivered almonds
- ☐ 1 1/8 C. sugar
- ☐ 2 C. brown sugar
- ☐ 1 C. pineapple juice
- ☐ 2 C. sangria wine
- ☐ 3/4 C. chopped macadamia nuts
- ☐ 1 T. baking powder
- ☐ 3 C. flour
- ☐ 4 C. chicken broth
- ☐ 1 T. white vinegar

Breakfast
Day One:

Breakfast Tarts

Makes 4 servings

1 (11 oz.) pkg. pie crust
   mix
12 slices bacon
1 C. shredded Cheddar
   cheese

4 eggs
1/4 C. milk
1/4 tsp. nutmeg
1/4 tsp. pepper

Preheat oven to 425°. Prepare pastry for a one crust pie according to package directions. Divide pastry into 4 equal parts and roll each part into a 6" circle. Place each pastry circle in a large muffin cup or 6 ounce pastry cup, making pleats so the pastry covers the bottoms and sides of each cup. Poke the surface of each crust with a fork and bake in oven for 8 to 10 minutes, until crusts are lightly browned. Remove crust from oven and reduce oven temperature to 350°. Meanwhile, in a medium skillet over medium high heat, cook bacon until browned. Remove bacon from skillet and drain on paper towels. Crumble 2 slices bacon into the bottom of each crust and sprinkle with 1/4 cup of the shredded Cheddar cheese.* Break 1 egg into each crust and pour 1 tablespoon milk into each crust. Sprinkle nutmeg and pepper over each tart and return to oven for an additional 15 to 20 minutes, until eggs are soft cooked.
*Reserve remaining 4 slices cooked bacon for Dinner on Day 3.

Lunch
Day One:

California Cabbage Salad

Makes 4 to 6 servings

**1 (3 oz.) pkg. chicken
flavored ramen noodles**
1/4 C. butter
1/2 C. sesame seeds
1/2 C. slivered almonds
**1 large head Napa
cabbage, shredded**

6 green onions, chopped
1/4 C. vegetable oil
1/4 C. rice wine vinegar
1 T. soy sauce
1 T. sesame oil
1/8 C. sugar

Crush the ramen noodles. In a medium skillet over medium heat, place butter. When butter has melted, stir in crushed ramen noodles, sesame seeds and slivered almonds. Stir until noodles, seeds and almonds are lightly toasted, stirring frequently to prevent burning. Add seasoning mix from ramen noodles and mix well. In a large bowl, place shredded cabbage and chopped green onions. Add flavored noodles, sesame seeds and slivered almonds. In a medium bowl, whisk together vegetable oil, rice wine vinegar, soy sauce, sesame oil and sugar. Whisk thoroughly, until sugar is dissolved. Pour mixture over salad and toss until evenly coated.

*Begin baking ham 3 hours prior to dinner (see page 74).

Dinner
Day One:

Sangria Ham

Makes 4 to 6 servings

1 (10 lb.) bone-in ham　　**1 C. pineapple juice**
1/4 C. whole cloves　　　**2 C. sangria wine**
2 C. brown sugar

Preheat oven to 400°. Using a sharp knife, score the ham 1/4" deep in a diamond pattern. Place ham in a large roaster and press cloves into ham. Pack a thick layer of brown sugar over the top of the ham as thickly as possible. Some brown sugar may fall off into the pan. Roast ham in oven, uncovered, for 20 minutes. Meanwhile, in a medium bowl, combine pineapple juice and sangria wine. When sugar begins to melt on ham, pour 1 cup of the wine mixture over ham and return ham to oven for 1 hour. After 1 hour, baste the ham with the remaining wine mixture and return ham to oven for an additional 2 hours. During final 1 hour of baking time, reduce oven temperature to 325° and baste ham every 20 minutes with the pan drippings. Ham is done when it reads 160* on a meat thermometer. To serve, cut slices of ham from the bone, setting aside all but 4 to 6 slices of the thick-cut ham.* Cut ham from the bone, leaving some of the ham on the bone and reserve.**
*Reserve most of the cooked ham slices (at least 6) for Breakfast on Day 2, Lunch on Day 3 and Dinner on Day 3.
**Reserve ham bone for Lunch on Day 3.

Breakfast
Day Two:

Ham & Cheese Casserole

Makes 4 servings

8 eggs
1 C. milk
Salt and pepper to taste
Leftover cooked ham from
    Dinner Day One

1 C. shredded Cheddar
    cheese

Preheat oven to 350°. In a large bowl, beat eggs until frothy. Add milk, salt and pepper and mix well. Dice 2 slices of leftover ham from Day 1 into small pieces.* Stir diced ham and shredded Cheddar cheese into egg mixture. Pour mixture into a 9x13" baking dish and bake in oven for 50 to 60 minutes, until top of casserole is lightly browned.

*Reserve remaining cooked ham for Lunch on Day 3 and Dinner on Day 3.

Lunch
Day Two:

American Tuna Hot Dish

Makes 4 to 6 servings

2 1/2 lbs. russet potatoes, peeled and cubed
1 C. milk
1/2 C. shredded mozzarella cheese
3 T. grated Parmesan cheese, divided

2 eggs
3 (6 oz.) cans chunk light tuna, drained
4 green onions, chopped

Preheat oven to 400°. In a large pot over high heat, place cubed potatoes and cover with water. Bring to a boil. Boil potatoes for 20 minutes, until tender. Drain pot and transfer all but 3 cups of the diced potatoes to a large bowl.* Add milk, shredded mozzarella cheese and 2 tablespoons Parmesan cheese. Using a hand mixer or potato masher, mash potatoes until almost smooth. Add beaten eggs and drained tuna to mashed potatoes and mix well. Fold in chopped green onions and season with salt and pepper to taste. Transfer mixture to a lightly greased 10" round pie pan. Top with remaining tablespoon grated Parmesan cheese. Bake in oven for 45 minutes, or until top of potatoes are golden brown.
*Reserve 3 cups diced cooked potatoes for Dinner on Day 3.

Dinner
Day Two:

Black Bean Burritos

Makes 4 burritos

4 (10") flour tortillas
4 T. vegetable oil
1 medium onion, chopped
1 red bell pepper, chopped
2 cloves garlic, minced
1 jalapeno pepper, seeded and minced

2 (15 oz.) cans black beans, drained and rinsed
1 (8 oz.) pkg. cream cheese, softened
1 tsp. salt
4 T. fresh chopped cilantro

Preheat oven to 350°. Wrap tortillas in aluminum foil and place in heated oven for 15 minutes. In a 10" skillet over medium heat, place vegetable oil. Add chopped onion, chopped red bell pepper, minced garlic and minced jalapeno pepper to skillet. Cook for 2 minutes, until softened, stirring occasionally. Add rinsed beans to skillet and cook for an additional 3 minutes. Cut cream cheese into cubes and add to skillet. Cook for 2 minutes, until cream cheese is melted, and stir in salt and cilantro. To assemble burritos, spoon a generous amount of the black bean mixture down the center of each warmed tortilla. Wrap tortillas to enclose filling and serve immediately.

Breakfast
Day Three:

Pineapple Bread

Makes 1 (5x9") loaf

3/4 C. chopped macadamia
　　nuts
4 eggs
1/2 C. vegetable oil
1 (20 oz.) can crushed
　　pineapple in juice

1 T. baking powder
3 C. flour
1 C. sugar

Preheat oven to 350°. Lightly grease a 5x9" loaf pan and line with waxed paper. In a large bowl, combine eggs, vegetable oil, crushed pineapple including pineapple juice from can and sugar. Mix well. Into a separate bowl, sift baking powder and flour. Stir flour mixture into pineapple mixture and stir until well combined. Fold in chopped macadamia nuts. Pour batter into prepared pan. Bake in oven for 50 to 60 minutes, or until a toothpick inserted in center of loaf comes out clean.
*Begin preparing soup 2 hours before Lunch (see page 79).

Lunch
Day Three:

Black Bean Soup

Makes 4 to 6 servings

2 (15 oz.) cans black beans, drained and rinsed
Leftover ham bone from Dinner Day One
6 C. water
4 C. chicken broth
1 T. salt

Leftover cooked ham from Breakfast Day Two
2 T. vegetable oil
1 small onion, chopped
1 tomato, diced
1 T. white vinegar

In a large pot over medium heat, combine rinsed black beans, ham bone, water, chicken broth and salt. Bring mixture to a simmer for 1 1/2 hours. Discard ham bone. In a blender or food processor, puree half of the mixture and return to pot with remaining mixture. Chop 2 slices leftover ham from Day 2 into small pieces.* In a medium skillet, place vegetable oil. Sauté ham slices, chopped onions and diced tomatoes in skillet until onions are softened. Stir in vinegar and add mixture to soup in pot. Let simmer for an additional 20 minutes. Ladle soup into bowls and serve hot.
*Reserve remaining cooked ham for Dinner.

Dinner
Day Three:

Camper's Casserole

Makes 4 to 6 servings

1 small head Napa
    cabbage, shredded
Leftover cooked bacon
    from Breakfast Day One
Leftover cooked ham
    from Lunch
1 onion, sliced

1 T. butter
Leftover diced cooked
    potatoes from Lunch
    Day Two
1/2 tsp. paprika
Salt and pepper to taste

In a medium saucepan over medium heat, place shredded cabbage and 1/2 cup water. Cook for 5 minutes, until cabbage is tender. Drain cabbage and set aside. Crumble leftover bacon from Day 1 into small pieces and chop leftover cooked ham from Lunch into small pieces. In a large skillet, place crumbled bacon and sliced onions, cooking until onions are softened. Add chopped ham, butter, cooked cabbage and leftover diced cooked potatoes from Day 2. Mix well and season with paprika, salt and pepper. Cook until mixture browns on the bottom, turn over in skillet and cook until browned on other side.

Trip Nine

SHOPPING LIST

Dairy & Eggs:
- ❑ 4 1/2 sticks butter
- ❑ 9 eggs
- ❑ 2 1/2 C. half n' half
- ❑ 1/2 C. shredded Swiss cheese
- ❑ 2 T. grated Parmesan cheese
- ❑ 1/2 C. milk
- ❑ 1/2 C. evaporated milk
- ❑ 2 C. buttermilk

Fruits & Vegetables:
- ❑ 3 (3 1/2 oz.) pkgs. shiitake mushrooms
- ❑ 3 cloves garlic
- ❑ 3 small onions (1 red)
- ❑ 3 red bell peppers
- ❑ 3 Roma tomatoes
- ❑ 1 small piece gingerroot
- ❑ 6 green onions
- ❑ 1 green bell pepper
- ❑ 1 small head romaine lettuce
- ❑ 1 small lemon

Breads & Grains:
- ❑ 1 (15 oz.) pkg. single crust refrigerated pie crust
- ❑ 2 (12 oz.) pkgs. angel hair pasta
- ❑ 4 1/2 C. long grain white rice
- ❑ 1 (1/4 oz.) pkg. dry active yeast
- ❑ 1 C. Bisquick baking mix

Meats:
- ❑ 12 slices bacon
- ❑ 6 (6 oz.) cans crabmeat
- ❑ 2 lbs. large shrimp
- ❑ 2 (3 or 4 lb.) whole chickens
- ❑ 1 lb. smoked sausage

Spices, Oils & Sauces:
- ❑ Salt and Pepper
- ❑ Nutmeg and Allspice
- ❑ Cayenne pepper
- ❑ 1 T. olive oil
- ❑ Dried parsley flakes
- ❑ 1 small bottle vegetable oil
- ❑ Dried thyme
- ❑ Dried oregano
- ❑ Cinnamon
- ❑ 1 small bottle soy sauce
- ❑ 2 T. sesame oil
- ❑ Dried cilantro
- ❑ Dried sage and Paprika
- ❑ Poultry seasoning
- ❑ 1/2 tsp. Dijon mustard
- ❑ Worcestershire sauce
- ❑ Hot pepper sauce
- ❑ 1 bay leaf

Others:
- ❑ 1 C. sugar
- ❑ 2 1/2 C. chicken broth
- ❑ 1/4 C. white wine
- ❑ 7 1/2 C. flour
- ❑ 2 C. brown sugar
- ❑ 3 C. chopped pecans
- ❑ 1 T. baking powder
- ❑ 1/2 tsp. baking soda
- ❑ 3 T. apple cider vinegar
- ❑ 1 T. honey

Breakfast
Day One:

Seafood Quiche

Makes 6 to 8 servings

8 slices bacon
1 (15 oz.) pkg. single crust refrigerated pie crust
1 T. butter
4 eggs
2 C. half n' half
1 tsp. salt
Pinch of sugar
Pinch of nutmeg
Pinch of cayenne pepper
Pinch of pepper
1/2 C. shredded Swiss cheese
6 (6 oz.) cans crabmeat, shredded
2 lbs. large shrimp
3 (3 1/2 oz.) pkgs. shiitake mushrooms

Preheat oven to 450°. In a large skillet over medium high heat, cook bacon until browned. Remove bacon to paper towels to drain. Crumble bacon and set aside. Line a 9" pie pan with refrigerated pie crust. In a small microwave-safe bowl, place butter. Melt butter in microwave and brush over pie crust in pan. Sprinkle crumbled bacon into pie crust. In a medium bowl, whisk together eggs, half n' half, salt, sugar, nutmeg, cayenne pepper and pepper. Mix well and pour over bacon in pie crust. Sprinkle shredded Swiss cheese and shredded crabmeat over egg mixture in pie crust. Peel and devein the shrimp and chop into pieces. Place all but 1/2 cup of the chopped shrimp in an airtight container.* Add remaining 1/2 cup chopped shrimp to egg mixture in pie crust. Clean and slice shiitake mushrooms. Arrange 1/3 of the shiitake mushrooms over mixture in pie crust.** Bake in oven for 10 minutes. Reduce oven temperature to 350° and bake for an additional 25 to 30 minutes. Remove quiche from oven and let sit for 10 minutes before serving.
*Reserve remaining chopped shrimp for Dinner on Day 3.
**Reserve remaining 2/3 of the sliced shiitake mushrooms for Lunch.

Shiitake Mushroom Pasta Dish

2 (12 oz.) pkgs. angel
   hair pasta
Leftover shiitake
   mushrooms from
   Breakfast
1 clove garlic, minced
1 small onion, chopped
1/4 C. white wine

1 T. olive oil
1/4 C. chicken broth
1/2 C. half n' half
Salt and pepper to taste
2 T. grated Parmesan
   cheese
2 tsp. dried parsley flakes

In a medium skillet over medium heat, sauté minced garlic and chopped onions in olive oil. Add 1/2 of the leftover sliced mushrooms from Breakfast and mix well.* Add chicken broth and wine, cooking until mixture reduces by half. Mix in half n' half and season with salt and pepper to taste. Meanwhile, in a large pot of lightly salted water, cook angel hair pasta according to package directions, for 6 to 8 minutes, until al dente. Drain pasta and transfer half of the cooked pasta to an airtight container.** In a large bowl, place remaining half of the cooked pasta. Pour mushroom mixture over pasta and toss until evenly coated. To serve, place pasta and sauce on plates and sprinkle some of the grated Parmesan cheese and some of the dried parsley flakes over each serving.

*Reserve remaining half of the sliced shiitake mushrooms for Lunch on Day 2.

** Reserve half of the cooked angel hair pasta for Dinner on Day 3.

Dinner
Day One:

New Orleans Chicken

Makes 4 servings

1 (3 or 4 lb.) whole chicken, skin removed	**1 tsp. brown sugar**
1/3 C. flour	**3/4 tsp. dried thyme**
1 T. vegetable oil	**3/4 tsp. dried oregano**
1/2 lb. smoked sausage	**1/2 tsp. salt**
2 cloves garlic, minced	**1/4 tsp. allspice**
1 onion, chopped	**1 1/2 C. long grain white rice**
2 red bell pepper, chopped	**2 1/4 C. chicken broth**
3 Roma tomatoes, chopped	

Cut chicken into pieces and set aside half of the pieces.* Dredge remaining half of the chicken pieces in flour. In a large saucepan over medium heat, place vegetable oil. Brown chicken pieces in saucepan for 8 minutes per side. Transfer browned chicken to a plate. Add smoked sausage, minced garlic, chopped onions, chopped red bell peppers, chopped tomatoes, brown sugar, thyme, oregano, salt and allspice to saucepan. Cook for 10 minutes, stirring occasionally, until peppers are softened. Stir in rice and chicken broth. Lay browned chicken pieces in rice mixture in skillet. Bring to a boil, reduce heat and cover. Let cook for 25 minutes, until liquid is absorbed and juices run clear.

*Reserve half of the chicken pieces for Lunch on Day 2.

**Begin making cinnamon buns for tomorrow's breakfast at least 2 1/2 hours prior to breakfast (see page 85).

Gooey Cinnamon Buns

Makes 12 cinnamon buns

1/4 C. plus 1 tsp. sugar, divided
1 (1/4 oz.) pkg. dry active yeast
1/2 C. warm water (110° F)
1/2 C. milk
1 1/4 C. butter, divided
1 tsp. salt
2 eggs, beaten
4 C. flour
1 1/2 C. brown sugar, divided
1 C. chopped pecans, divided
1 T. cinnamon

In a small bowl, dissolve 1 teaspoon sugar and yeast in warm water. Let stand until creamy, about 10 minutes. In a small saucepan over low heat, heat milk until warmed and mix in 1/4 cup sugar, 1/4 cup butter and salt. Stir until butter is melted. Remove from heat and let mixture cool to lukewarm. In a large bowl, combine yeast mixture, milk mixture, eggs and 1 1/2 cups flour. Stir until well combined and mix in remaining 2 1/2 cups flour, 1/2 cup at a time, beating well after each addition. When mixture forms a dough, turn dough out onto a lightly floured surface. Knead dough until smooth, about 8 minutes. Lightly oil a large bowl and place dough in the bowl, turning to cover dough with oil. Cover bowl with a damp cloth and let dough rise for 1 hour. Meanwhile, in a small saucepan over medium heat, place 3/4 cup butter. When butter has melted, stir in 3/4 cup brown sugar, whisking until well mixed. Pour mixture into the bottom of 9x13" baking dish. Sprinkle 1/2 cup of the chopped pecans over the bottom of the baking dish. In a small, microwave-safe bowl, melt remaining 1/4 cup butter and set aside. In a separate small bowl, combine remaining 3/4 cup brown sugar, remaining 1/2 cup pecans and cinnamon. Turn dough out onto a lightly floured surface and roll into a 14x18" rectangle. Brush half of the melted butter over dough to within 1/2" of the edge and sprinkle brown sugar mixture over dough. Starting at one side of the dough, tightly roll dough into a log, pinching the seams to seal. Brush remaining melted butter over the dough and cut the log into 12 rounds. Place the rounds, cut side down in the prepared pan. Cover dough and let rise for 1 hour, until buns are doubled in size. Preheat oven to 375°. Bake in oven for 25 to 30 minutes, until golden brown. Remove from oven and let cool slightly before inverting buns onto a serving plate, scraping remaining filling from pan onto the rolls.
*Begin marinating chicken and sausage for Lunch (see page 86).

Chicken Fried Rice

Makes 4 servings

**Leftover chicken from
   Dinner Day One**
1/2 lb. smoked sausage
1 tsp. salt
1 T. soy sauce
2 T. sesame oil
**1 small piece gingerroot,
   chopped**

**Leftover sliced mushrooms
   from Lunch Day One**
3 C. long grain white rice
2 1/2 C. water
2 tsp. dried cilantro
6 green onions, chopped

Cut leftover chicken pieces from Day 1 and smoked sausages into small pieces. In a large ziplock bag, place chicken pieces, smoked sausage pieces, salt and soy sauce. Let marinate in refrigerator for 4 hours. In a large saucepan, skillet or wok over medium high heat, place sesame oil. Add marinated chicken and sausage pieces and cook, stirring frequently, until browned. Add chopped gingerroot and leftover sliced mushrooms from Day 1. Cook for an additional 3 minutes, stirring frequently. Stir in rice and season with salt and pepper. If available, transfer entire mixture to a rice cooker and add water. Heat until rice is tender and stir in cilantro and green onions. If not using a rice cooker, add water to saucepan, skillet or wok, cover and reduce heat to medium low. Let cook, stirring frequently, until rice is tender. When rice has absorbed all of the liquid, add cilantro and chopped green onions and toss until well incorporated.

Dinner
Day Two:

Oven Fried Chicken

Makes 4 to 6 servings

1/3 tsp. butter	1/2 tsp. poultry seasoning
1 C. Bisquick baking mix	1/2 tsp. dried sage
1/3 C. chopped pecans	1/2 C. evaporated milk
2 tsp. paprika	1 (3 or 4 lb.) whole chicken,
1/2 tsp. salt	cut into 8 pieces

Preheat oven to 350°. Lightly grease a 9x13" baking dish and set aside. In a small microwave-safe bowl, place butter. Heat butter in microwave until melted and set aside. In a shallow dish, combine baking mix, chopped pecans, paprika, salt, poultry seasoning and dried sage. Mix well. Place evaporated milk in a separate shallow dish. Dip chicken pieces in evaporated milk and roll in pecan mixture until fully coated. Place coated chicken pieces in prepared baking dish and drizzle with melted butter. Bake in oven for 1 hour, or until juices run clear. Remove 2 or 3 pieces of the fried chicken, wrap and refrigerate.*
Place remaining fried chicken pieces on a serving plate and serve.
*Reserve 2 or 3 fried chicken pieces for Lunch on Day 3.

Breakfast
Day Three:

Pecan Waffles

Makes 4 servings

1/3 C. butter	3 eggs, separated
3 C. flour	2 C. buttermilk
1 T. baking powder	1/2 C. vegetable oil
1/4 C. sugar	1 2/3 C. chopped pecans
1/2 tsp. baking soda	

Preheat waffle iron. In a small microwave-safe bowl, place butter. Heat in microwave until butter is melted and set aside. Into a large bowl, sift flour, baking powder, sugar and baking soda. In a separate bowl, whisk together egg yolks and buttermilk. Add buttermilk mixture, melted butter and vegetable oil to flour mixture, stirring gently until well combined. In a separate bowl, using a hand mixer, beat egg whites until stiff peaks form. Fold egg whites into batter. Spray waffle iron with non-stick cooking spray and pour 1/4 of the batter onto hot waffle iron. Sprinkle a generous amount of the chopped pecans over the batter and close waffle iron. Cook until golden brown. Repeat with remaining batter and chopped pecans.

Lunch
Day Three:

Southern Fried
Chicken Salad

Makes 4 servings

**Leftover fried chicken
from Dinner Day Two**
1 red bell pepper, chopped
**1 green bell pepper,
chopped**
1 small red onion, chopped
**1 small head romaine lettuce,
rinsed and shredded**

4 slices bacon
3 T. apple cider vinegar
1 T. honey
1/2 tsp. Dijon mustard
1/2 tsp. salt
1/4 tsp. pepper

Cut leftover fried chicken from Day 2 into small pieces, discarding the bones. In a large bowl, combine chopped red bell pepper, chopped green bell pepper, chopped red onions, shredded lettuce and fried chicken pieces. In a medium skillet over medium high heat, cook bacon until browned and remove bacon to paper towels to drain. Remove all but 2 tablespoons of the bacon drippings from the skillet. To bacon drippings, add apple cider vinegar, honey, Dijon mustard, salt and pepper. Bring mixture to a low boil, stirring frequently, and pour over ingredients in bowl. Crumbled drained bacon over salad and toss until well incorporated.

Dinner
Day Three:

Creole Shrimp & Pasta

Makes 4 servings

**Leftover cooked pasta from
    Lunch Day One**
7 T. butter
1 T. Worcestershire sauce
Hot pepper sauce to taste
Juice of 1 small lemon

1 bay leaf
1/2 tsp. dried thyme
3 T. vegetable oil
**Leftover chopped shrimp
    from Breakfast Day One**
1 T. dried parsley flakes

In a large microwave-safe bowl, place leftover cooked angel hair pasta from Day 1. Heat pasta briefly in microwave until just warmed. In a small saucepan over low heat, place butter. When butter has melted, stir in Worcestershire sauce and hot sauce. Mix well and stir in lemon juice, bay leaf and dried thyme. Heat mixture, being careful not to let simmer. In a large skillet over medium high heat, place vegetable oil. Add chopped shrimp and sauté shrimp for 3 to 4 minutes, until shrimp turns pink. Discard all but 1 tablespoon of the cooking liquid from skillet. Discard bay leaf from butter mixture and pour butter mixture over shrimp in skillet. Mix well and stir in dried parsley. To serve, divide cooked angel hair pasta among four plates. Drizzle shrimp sauce over pasta.

Trip Ten

SHOPPING LIST

Dairy & Eggs:
- ❑ 4 1/2 C. milk
- ❑ 15 eggs
- ❑ 3 sticks butter
- ❑ 2 C. shredded Swiss cheese
- ❑ 1/2 C. shredded Cheddar cheese

Fruits & Vegetables:
- ❑ 3 green onions
- ❑ 8 large potatoes
- ❑ 4 large carrots
- ❑ 1 onion
- ❑ 1 C. fresh blueberries
- ❑ 3 (10 oz.) cans mixed vegetables

Meats:
- ❑ 10 slices bacon
- ❑ 10 boneless, skinless chicken breasts
- ❑ 1 (4 lb.) beef chuck roast

Breads & Grains:
- ❑ 4 slices bread
- ❑ 2 1/2 C. dry bread crumbs
- ❑ 4 French sandwich rolls
- ❑ 2 (9") deep dish frozen pie crusts

Spices, Oils & Sauces:
- ❑ Salt and Pepper
- ❑ Dried parsley flakes
- ❑ Onion salt
- ❑ Garlic salt
- ❑ 3 (3/4 oz.) pkgs. brown gravy mix
- ❑ 1 small bottle barbecue sauce
- ❑ 2 T. Worcestershire sauce
- ❑ 2 C. corn oil

Others:
- ❑ 1 C. sugar
- ❑ 1/4 C. brown sugar
- ❑ 2 1/2 C. flour
- ❑ 2 1/2 tsp. baking powder
- ❑ 1 (10 1/2 oz.) can beef broth
- ❑ 1 1/2 T. sesame seeds
- ❑ 1 (10 3/4 oz.) can cream of chicken soup

Breakfast
Day One:

Swiss Cheese Scramble

Makes 4 to 6 servings

8 slices bacon	**Salt and pepper to taste**
4 slices bread, cubed	**1/2 C. butter, divided**
2 3/4 C. milk	**2 C. shredded Swiss cheese**
8 eggs	**1 C. dry bread crumbs**

In a large skillet over medium high heat, cook bacon until browned and remove bacon to paper towels drain. Drain skillet of fat. Crumble bacon and set aside. In a large bowl, combine bread cubes and milk. Let soak for 5 minutes and drain milk into a separate bowl. Add eggs, salt and pepper to milk and whisk until well blended. In the same skillet over medium heat, place 1/4 cup butter. Heat until butter is melted and add egg mixture to skillet. Scramble eggs until slightly cooked, but not hard. Add soaked bread cubes and transfer mixture to a greased 9x13" baking dish. Sprinkle shredded Swiss cheese over mixture in baking dish. In a small microwave-safe bowl, place remaining 1/4 cup butter. Heat in microwave until butter is melted. Add dry bread crumbs to melted butter and toss until well blended. Sprinkle bread crumb mixture over egg mixture in baking dish. Cover and chill in refrigerator for 30 minutes. Preheat oven to 350°. Bake in oven for 40 minutes and serve warm.

Lunch
Day One:

Chicken Croquettes

Makes 4 servings

**6 boneless, skinless
  chicken breasts
1 1/2 C. dry bread crumbs
2 or 3 eggs, lightly beaten**

**3 green onions, chopped
1/2 T. dried parsley flakes
1 tsp. salt
1/2 tsp pepper**

In a large skillet over medium high heat, cook chicken breasts until cooked throughout and no longer pink. Remove chicken from skillet, let cool and chop into small pieces. Set aside half of the chopped chicken in an airtight container.* In a large bowl, combine remaining half of the chopped chicken, bread crumbs, beaten eggs and chopped green onions. Mix well. If mixture is too dry, add another egg and mix well. Stir in parsley flakes, salt and pepper and mix well. Form mixture into 4 patties. In the same skillet, heat vegetable oil and fry patties in skillet until golden brown on both sides, turning once.

*Reserve half of the cooked chopped chicken for Dinner on Day 3.
**Begin preparing pot roast at least 2 to 3 hours before Dinner.

Dinner
Day One:

Garlic Pot Roast

Makes 4 servings

1 (4 lb.) beef chuck roast
1/2 C. butter
1 T. onion salt
1 T. garlic salt
1/4 C. sugar
1/4 C. brown sugar
3 (3/4 oz.) pkgs. brown
    gravy mix

4 large potatoes, peeled
    and diced
4 large carrots, peeled
    and diced
1 onion, sliced
2 C. water

Preheat oven to 325°. Lightly coat the beef chuck roast with butter. Sprinkle onion salt, garlic salt, sugar, brown sugar and 1 package of brown gravy mix over roast. In a large roasting pan, evenly spread diced potatoes, diced carrots and half of the sliced onions.* Sprinkle 1 package brown gravy mix over vegetables and place roast over potatoes and carrots. Sprinkle remaining brown gravy mix over roast and vegetables in pan. Add water and any remaining butter to pan. Cover roasting pan and bake in oven for 30 minutes. Reduce temperature to 300° and continue to bake for 2 hours and 15 minutes, or until roast reaches desired doneness. Remove roast from oven and cut into slices. Set aside all but 4 to 6 large slices of roast.** Place remaining 4 to 6 slices, carrots and potatoes on a serving platter and serve.

*Reserve half of the onion slices for Breakfast on Day 3.
**Reserve most of the cooked roast for Lunch on Day 2 and Lunch on Day 3.

Breakfast
Day Two:

Blueberry
Breakfast Muffins

Makes 12 muffins

1 3/4 C. flour	**3/4 C. milk**
1/3 C. sugar	**1 egg**
2 1/2 tsp. baking powder	**1/3 C. butter**
1/2 tsp. salt	**1 C. fresh blueberries**

Preheat oven to 400°. Lightly grease 12 muffin cups and set aside. In a large bowl, whisk together flour, sugar, baking powder and salt. In a small microwave-safe bowl, place butter. Heat butter in microwave until melted. Add milk, egg and melted butter to flour mixture. Stir just until dry ingredients are moistened. Fold in fresh blueberries and pour batter into prepared muffin cups. Bake in oven for 20 to 25 minutes, or until a toothpick inserted in center of muffins comes out clean. Serve warm.

*Begin preparing stew at least 1 hour before Lunch (see page 96).

Lunch
Day Two:

Roast Brunswick Stew

**Leftover cooked roast
 from Dinner Day One
2 (10 oz.) cans mixed
 vegetables in liquid**

**2 1/2 C. barbecue sauce
2 T. Worcestershire sauce
1 (10 1/2 oz.) can beef
 broth**

Shred half of the leftover cooked roast from Day 1.* In a slow cooker or large roasting pan, place shredded roast, mixed vegetables with liquid, barbecue sauce, Worcestershire sauce and beef broth. Mix lightly and cover. If using a slow cooker, cook on High setting for 1 hour. If using a roasting pan, cook over low heat for 1 hour, stirring frequently. When soup is done, strain 2 cups of the broth mixture into an airtight container and refrigerate.** Ladle remaining soup into bowls.

*Reserve remaining cooked roast slices for Lunch on Day 3.
**Reserve strained broth mixture for Lunch on Day 3.

Dinner
Day Two:

Chicken Nuggets

4 boneless, skinless
   chicken breasts
2 C. corn oil
1 egg, beaten

1/3 C. water
1/3 C. flour
1 1/2 T. sesame seeds
1 1/2 tsp. salt

Rinse chicken breast under cold water and pat dry with paper towels. Cut chicken into 1" square pieces. Place corn oil in a deep pot and place pot over medium heat. In a small bowl, combine beaten egg and water. Stir in flour, sesame seeds and salt. Mix well until a smooth batter forms. Dip chicken pieces in batter and drain off any excess. Add battered chicken pieces, a few at a time, to hot oil in pot. Fry for about 4 minutes or until golden brown. Remove chicken from oil and make sure the pieces have been cooked throughout and are no longer pink in the middle. Drain chicken pieces on paper towels before serving.

Breakfast
Day Three:

Cheesy Hash Browns

Makes 4 servings

Leftover onion from
    Dinner Day One
2 slices bacon
2 T. butter
4 large potatoes, peeled
    and shredded
	Salt and pepper to taste
	2 eggs
	1/2 C. shredded Cheddar
	    cheese

Chop leftover onion slices from Day 1 into small pieces. In a large skillet over medium high heat, cook bacon until browned and remove to paper towels to drain, leaving bacon grease in pan. Crumble bacon and set aside. Return skillet to medium heat and stir butter into bacon drippings. Add chopped onions and shredded potatoes. Cover pan and cook, stirring frequently, until potatoes are golden brown. Crack eggs over potatoes and stir until combined. Sprinkle with salt, pepper and shredded Cheddar cheese. Continue to cook until eggs are set and cheese is melted.

Lunch
Day Three:

French Dip Sandwiches

Makes 4 sandwiches

**Leftover cooked roast
from Lunch Day Two
Leftover strained broth
from Lunch Day Two**

4 French sandwich rolls

Shred leftover cooked roast from Day 2 or cut into thin slices. Place slices on a plate and reheat in microwave just until warmed. Place leftover strained broth from Day 2 in a microwave-safe bowl and reheat in microwave until warmed, being careful not to boil. To assemble sandwiches, place 1/4 of the heated roast slices on each sandwich roll. Serve with heated broth mixture for dipping.

Dinner
Day Three:

Chicken Pot Pie

Makes 4 to 6 servings

2 (9") deep dish frozen pie crusts, thawed
1 (10 oz.) can mixed vegetables, drained
Leftover cooked chopped chicken from Lunch Day One

1 (10 3/4 oz.) can cream of chicken soup
1/2 C. milk

Preheat oven to 350°. In a medium bowl, combine drained vegetables, leftover cooked chopped chicken from Day 1, cream of chicken soup and milk. Pour mixture into one of the frozen pie crusts. Turn the other crust over the filled pie crust and pop out of the tin to cover the filled pie. Seal the edges by pressing down with a fork and poke holes in the top crust. Bake in oven for 30 minutes, or until crust is golden brown.

Trip Eleven

SHOPPING LIST

Dairy & Eggs:
- ❑ 1 (12 oz.) pkg. cream cheese
- ❑ 2 1/2 C. milk
- ❑ 5 eggs
- ❑ 1/2 C. shredded Swiss cheese
- ❑ 1 stick butter
- ❑ 1/2 C. shredded Cheddar cheese
- ❑ 1 (6 oz.) carton plain yogurt
- ❑ 1/4 C. evaporated milk
- ❑ 1/4 C. grated Parmesan cheese

Fruits & Vegetables:
- ❑ 4 green onions
- ❑ 2 onions (1 small)
- ❑ 1 green bell pepper
- ❑ 3 Roma tomatoes
- ❑ 1 (12 oz.) pkg. frozen stir-fry vegetables
- ❑ 1 (8 3/4 oz.) can whole kernel corn
- ❑ 2 cloves garlic
- ❑ 2 (15 oz.) cans kidney beans
- ❑ 1 (28 oz.) can crushed tomatoes

Meats:
- ❑ 12 slices bacon
- ❑ 3 1/2 lbs. ground beef
- ❑ 8 boneless, skinless chicken breasts

Breads & Grains:
- ❑ 1 (10 oz.) can refrigerated flaky biscuit dough
- ❑ 2 C. Bisquick baking mix
- ❑ 1/4 C. dry bread crumbs
- ❑ 4 (10") flour tortillas, optional

Spices, Oils & Sauces:
- ❑ Salt and Pepper
- ❑ Paprika
- ❑ Curry powder
- ❑ 1/4 C. plus 3 T. Dijon mustard
- ❑ 1 small bottle vegetable oil
- ❑ Nutmeg
- ❑ Vanilla
- ❑ Fajita seasoning
- ❑ Dried cilantro
- ❑ Chili powder

Others:
- ❑ 1 (10 3/4 oz.) can tomato soup
- ❑ 1/2 C. ketchup
- ❑ 1 1/2 C. brown sugar
- ❑ 1/4 C. honey
- ❑ 2 T. apricot jam
- ❑ 1/4 C. powdered sugar
- ❑ 1 C. chopped walnuts
- ❑ 1/3 C. maple syrup
- ❑ 1/2 C. 2 T. sugar
- ❑ 1 1/2 C. pizza sauce
- ❑ 2 C. flour
- ❑ 1 C. whole wheat flour
- ❑ 1 tsp. baking soda
- ❑ 2 tsp. baking powder
- ❑ 1 T. distilled white vinegar

Breakfast
Day One:

Bacon Quiche Tarts

Makes 10 tarts

12 slices bacon	**1/2 C. shredded Swiss**
1 (12 oz.) pkg. cream	**cheese**
cheese, softened	**4 green onions, chopped**
2 T. milk	**1 (10 oz.) can refrigerated**
2 eggs	**flaky biscuit dough**

Preheat oven to 375°. Lightly grease 10 muffin cups and set aside. In a large skillet over medium high heat, cook bacon until browned. Remove bacon to paper towels to drain. Crumble bacon and place half of the crumbled bacon in an airtight container in refrigerator.* In a medium bowl, combine 3/4 of the cream cheese**, milk and eggs. Using a hand mixer, beat ingredients together until smooth. Fold in shredded Swiss cheese and chopped green onions and set aside. Separate biscuit dough into 10 biscuits. Press 1 biscuit into the bottom and up sides of each muffin cup. Sprinkle half of the crumbled bacon into the bottoms of the filled muffin cups and spoon 2 tablespoons of the cream cheese mixture into each muffin cup. Bake in oven for 20 to 25 minutes, until filling is set and crust is golden brown. Sprinkle remaining half of the crumbled bacon over each muffin cup and press lightly into the filling. Remove tarts from muffin cups and serve warm.

*Reserve half of the crumbled bacon for Lunch on Day 2.
**Reserve remaining 1/4 of the cream cheese for Breakfast on Day 2.

Lunch
Day One:

BBQ Sloppy Joes

Makes 4 to 6 servings

3 1/2 lbs. ground beef
1 (10 3/4 oz.) can tomato soup

1/2 C. ketchup
1/2 C. brown sugar

In a large skillet over medium heat, place ground beef. Cook ground beef until browned and drain skillet of fat. Place all but 3 cups of the cooked ground beef in an airtight container and refrigerate.* Add tomato soup and stir until well mixed. Add 1/4 soup can of water, ketchup and brown sugar and mix thoroughly. Let mixture simmer for 30 minutes. To serve, spoon ground beef mixture onto buns.
*Reserve most of the cooked ground beef for Lunch on Day 2 and Dinner on Day 3.

Dinner
Day One:

Honey Mustard Chicken

Makes 6 to 8 servings

**6 boneless, skinless
 chicken breasts**
1 tsp. paprika
1/4 tsp. pepper

1/2 tsp. curry powder
3 T. Dijon mustard
1/4 C. honey
2 T. apricot jam

Preheat oven to 350°. In a large skillet over medium high heat, cook chicken breasts until heated throughout and no longer pink. May have to cook chicken in batches. Once 2 chicken breasts have been cooked, wrap the two cooked chicken breasts and place in refrigerator.* Sprinkle remaining 4 chicken breasts with paprika, pepper and curry powder. Place in a large baking dish. In a small bowl, combine Dijon mustard, honey and apricot jam. Mix well and pour mixture over chicken in baking dish. Chill in refrigerator for 30 minutes. Bake chicken in oven, basting often with juices, for 1 hour.
*Reserve 2 cooked chicken breasts for Lunch on Day 3.

Breakfast
Day Two:

Maple Twists

Makes 16 rolls

**Leftover cream cheese
from Breakfast Day One**
1/4 C. powdered sugar
2 T. butter, softened
1 C. brown sugar
1/2 C. chopped walnuts

1/3 C. maple syrup
2 C. Bisquick baking mix
1/4 C. milk
2 T. sugar
1 egg

Preheat oven to 425°. In a medium bowl, combine leftover cream cheese from Day 1, powdered sugar and butter. Mix well and set aside. In a 9x13" baking dish, combine brown sugar, chopped walnuts and maple syrup. Mix well and spread evenly over bottom of baking dish. In a separate medium bowl, combine baking mix, milk, sugar and egg until a dough forms. Beat dough vigorously until mixture is smooth. Round dough into a ball and knead 8 times on a lightly floured flat surface. Roll the dough into a 9x16" rectangle. Spread cream cheese mixture over dough and carefully fold up sides of dough into thirds. Press edges of dough to seal. Cut dough into 16 1" strips. Gently twist each strip and place twisted strips in baking dish over brown sugar mixture. Bake in oven for 15 minutes. To serve, invert strips onto a serving plate.

Lunch
Day Two:

Upside Down Pizza

Makes 4 to 6 servings

Leftover cooked ground beef from Lunch Day One
1 onion, chopped
1 green bell pepper, chopped
Leftover crumbled bacon from Breakfast Day One
1 1/2 C. pizza sauce

3 Roma tomatoes, chopped
1/2 C. shredded Cheddar cheese
2 eggs
1 C. milk
1 T. vegetable oil
1 C. flour
1/4 tsp. salt

Preheat oven to 400°. In a large skillet over medium high heat, place half of the leftover cooked ground beef from Day 1*, chopped onions, chopped green bell peppers. Sauté until ground beef is heated and onions are tender. Drain skillet of fat and stir in leftover crumbled bacon from Day 1 and pizza sauce. Transfer mixture to a 9x13" baking dish. Sprinkle chopped tomatoes and shredded Cheddar cheese over mixture in baking dish. In a medium bowl, lightly beat the eggs and mix in milk and vegetable oil. Stir in flour and salt and, using a hand mixer, beat at medium speed for 2 minutes. Pour mixture evenly over meat mixture in baking dish. Bake in oven for 20 to 30 minutes, or until topping is lightly puffed and golden brown. To serve, cut pizza casserole into squares and invert each serving onto a plate.
*Reserve remaining half of the cooked ground beef for Dinner on Day 3.

Dinner
Day Two:

Baked Parmesan Chicken

Makes 4 servings

1/4 C. Dijon mustard
1/4 C. evaporated milk
1/4 C. dry bread crumbs
1/4 C. grated Parmesan
    cheese

2 boneless, skinless chicken
    breasts

Preheat oven to 475°. Lightly grease a 9x13" baking dish and set aside. Cut each chicken breast in half and rinse under cold water. Pat dry and set on paper towels to drain. In a shallow bowl, combine Dijon mustard and evaporated milk, mixing until blended. In a separate shallow bowl, combine dry bread crumbs and grated Parmesan cheese, mixing until incorporated. Dip each chicken breast half in the mustard mixture and then in the bread crumb mixture until fully coated. Place coated chicken breast halves in prepared dish. Bake in oven for 15 to 20 minutes, until chicken is no longer pink in the middle and topping is golden brown.

Breakfast
Day Three:

Walnut Whole Wheat Muffins

Makes 12 muffins

1 C. flour
1 C. whole wheat flour
1/2 C. sugar
1 tsp. baking soda
2 tsp. baking powder
1 tsp. salt

1/2 tsp. nutmeg
1 (6 oz.) carton plain yogurt
1 C. milk
1 tsp. vanilla
1/2 C. chopped walnuts

Preheat oven to 375°. Lightly grease 12 muffin cups and set aside. In a large bowl, combine flour, whole wheat flour, sugar, baking soda, baking powder, salt and nutmeg. In a medium bowl, combine plain yogurt, milk and vanilla. Mix well and pour yogurt mixture over flour mixture and stir just until blended. Fold in chopped walnuts and mix lightly. Spoon batter into prepared muffins cups. Bake in oven for 18 to 20 minutes, or until a toothpick inserted in center of muffins comes out clean. Remove muffins from oven and let cool slightly on a wire rack.

Lunch
Day Three:

Southwest Chicken Stir-Fry

Makes 4 servings

2 T. butter
Leftover cooked chicken
    breast from Dinner
    Day One
2 1/2 tsp. fajita seasoning
1/4 tsp. salt
1 (12 oz.) pkg. frozen stir-fry
    vegetables, thawed

1 (8 3/4 oz.) can whole
    kernel corn, drained
1 tsp. dried cilantro
4 (10") flour tortillas,
    optional

In a large skillet over medium high heat, place butter. When butter has melted, stir in chicken pieces, fajita seasoning and salt. Cook for about 5 minutes, stirring occasionally, until heated throughout. Stir in thawed stir-fry vegetables, drained corn and cilantro and continue to cook, stirring occasionally. To serve, spoon mixture onto plate or serve inside warm tortillas.

Dinner
Day Three:

Delicious Chili

2 T. vegetable oil
Leftover cooked ground
   beef from Lunch
   Day Two
1 small onion, chopped
2 cloves garlic, minced

2 (15 oz.) cans kidney beans
1 (28 oz.) can crushed
   tomatoes in juice
2 T. chili powder
1 T. distilled white vinegar
Salt and pepper to taste

    In a 2-quart saucepan over medium high heat, place vegetable oil, leftover cooked ground beef from Day 2, chopped onions and minced garlic. Cook until ground beef is heated and vegetables are softened. Drain pan of fat and stir in kidney beans, crushed tomatoes in juice, chili powder and vinegar. Season with salt and pepper to taste. Bring chili to a boil, reduce heat, cover and let simmer for 30 minutes.

Trip Twelve

SHOPPING LIST

Dairy & Eggs:
- ❑ 1 1/2 sticks butter
- ❑ 9 eggs
- ❑ 1 1/2 C. milk
- ❑ 2 T. heavy cream
- ❑ 1 (3 oz.) pkg. cream cheese
- ❑ 1 C. shredded Cheddar cheese
- ❑ 1 C. shredded Monterey Jack cheese

Fruits & Vegetables:
- ❑ 6 cloves garlic
- ❑ 1 (29 oz.) can diced tomatoes
- ❑ 3 onions
- ❑ 8 black olives
- ❑ 1 head iceberg lettuce
- ❑ 3 green onions
- ❑ 1 (11 oz.) can mandarin oranges
- ❑ 1/2 C. raisins
- ❑ 2 green bell peppers
- ❑ 2 red bell peppers
- ❑ 1 (14 1/2 oz.) can mixed vegetables
- ❑ 1 (6 oz.) pkg. dried mixed fruit

Meats:
- ❑ 8 boneless, skinless chicken breasts
- ❑ 6 (4 oz.) salmon fillets

Breads & Grains:
- ❑ 5 C. old fashioned oats
- ❑ 8 (6") corn tortillas
- ❑ 1/2 C. dry bread crumbs
- ❑ 1 (8 oz.) pkg. rice noodles
- ❑ 4 C. uncooked white rice
- ❑ 10 (10") flour tortillas

Spices, Oils & Sauces:
- ❑ Salt and Pepper
- ❑ Cinnamon
- ❑ Vanilla
- ❑ 1 medium bottle vegetable oil
- ❑ Dried cilantro
- ❑ Cumin
- ❑ Chili powder
- ❑ 3 bay leaves
- ❑ Cayenne pepper
- ❑ 3 T. Dijon mustard
- ❑ Dried parsley flakes
- ❑ 4 T. olive oil
- ❑ 1 small bottle soy sauce
- ❑ 1 T. sesame oil
- ❑ 3 T. rice vinegar
- ❑ 1 (1 1/4 oz.) env. fajita seasoning
- ❑ Lemon pepper
- ❑ Garlic salt
- ❑ Paprika

Others:
- ❑ 1 C. chopped pecans
- ❑ 2 C. honey
- ❑ 7 C. chicken broth
- ❑ 2 T. brown sugar
- ❑ 1 T. sesame seeds
- ❑ 1 (10 3/4 oz.) can cream of chicken soup
- ❑ 1 (10 3/4 oz.) can cream of mushroom soup
- ❑ 1 C. cashews
- ❑ 1 C. powdered milk

Breakfast
Day One:

Honey Fruit Granola

Makes 5 1/2 cups

3 1/2 C. old fashioned oats
1/3 C. chopped pecans
4 T. butter
1/2 C. honey
1 tsp. vanilla

1/2 tsp. cinnamon
1/4 tsp. salt
1 (6 oz.) pkg. dried mixed
   fruit

Preheat oven to 350°. In a large bowl, combine oats and chopped pecans. Spread mixture evenly onto a 10x15" jellyroll pan. In a small microwave-safe bowl, place butter. Heat butter in microwave until melted. In a separate small bowl, combine melted butter, honey, vanilla, cinnamon and salt. Mix well and pour over oat mixture in pan. Toss until well mixed. Bake in oven for 30 to 35 minutes, stirring after every 10 minutes. Remove from oven and stir in chopped dried fruit. Let cool completely and serve dry, with milk or crumbled over yogurt.

Lunch
Day One:

Chicken Tortilla Soup

Makes 4 to 6 servings

8 boneless, skinless
   chicken breasts
6 T. vegetable oil
8 (6") corn tortillas,
   coarsely chopped
6 cloves garlic, minced
1 T. dried cilantro
1 onion, chopped

1 (29 oz.) can diced
   tomatoes
2 T. cumin
1 T. chili powder
3 bay leaves
6 C. chicken broth
1 tsp. salt
1/2 tsp. cayenne pepper

In a large skillet over medium high heat, cook chicken breasts until cooked throughout and no longer pink. May have to cook chicken in batches. When all chicken has been cooked, let cool slightly and chop into pieces. Place all but 2 cups of the chopped chicken in airtight container and refrigerate.* In a large pot over medium heat, place vegetable oil. Add chopped corn tortillas, minced garlic, cilantro and chopped onions. Sauté for 2 to 3 minutes and stir in diced tomatoes in juice. Bring mixture to a boil and add cumin, chili powder, bay leaves and chicken broth. Return to a boil, reduce heat and let simmer for 30 minutes. Stir in salt and cayenne pepper. Before serving, remove bay leaves and mix in remaining 2 cups cooked chopped chicken. Ladle soup into bowls.

*Reserve most of the cooked chopped chicken for Lunch on Day 2, Dinner on Day 2 and Lunch on Day 3.

Dinner
Day One:

Baked Salmon

1/4 C. butter	1/4 C. chopped pecans
3 T. Dijon mustard	2 tsp. dried parsley flakes
1 1/2 T. honey	6 (4 oz.) salmon fillets
1/4 C. dry bread crumbs	Salt and pepper to taste

Preheat oven to 400°. In a small microwave-safe bowl, place butter. Heat butter in microwave until melted. Remove from microwave and stir in Dijon mustard and honey. Mix well and set aside. In a separate bowl, combine bread crumbs, chopped pecans and dried parsley flakes. Place salmon fillets into a large baking dish. Brush each salmon fillet with the Dijon mixture and sprinkle some of the bread crumb mixture over each fillet. Bake in oven for 12 to 15 minutes, or until salmon flakes easily with a fork. Season with salt and pepper to taste. When salmon is done, remove from oven and place 2 of the baked fillets in an airtight container.* Place remaining 4 baked salmon fillets on a serving dish and serve.

*Reserve 2 baked salmon fillets for Breakfast on Day 2 and Dinner on Day 3.

Breakfast
Day Two:

Seafood Frittata

Makes 4 servings

4 T. olive oil	6 eggs
8 black olives, chopped	2 T. milk
1 onion, chopped	2 T. heavy cream
Salt and pepper to taste	1 (3 oz.) pkg. cream cheese,
Leftover baked salmon	cubed
from Dinner Day One	

Preheat oven to 350°. In a medium skillet over medium heat, place olive oil. Heat oil and stir in chopped olives and half of the chopped onions*, salt and pepper. Cook until onions are softened and add one baked salmon fillet**. Cook, pulling salmon apart with a fork. In a medium bowl, whisk together eggs, milk and heavy cream. Pour milk mixture over salmon mixture in skillet, stirring gently. Place cream cheese cubes over top. Continue to cook until egg begins to cook. Place skillet in oven for 20 minutes, until mixture is cooked and puffed. To serve, flip frittata onto a serving plate and cut into wedges.
*Reserve remaining half of the chopped onions for Dinner on Day 3.
**Reserve remaining baked salmon fillet for Dinner on Day 3.

Simple Mandarin Salad

Makes 6 servings

2 T. brown sugar	**Leftover cooked chopped**
2 tsp. soy sauce	**chicken from Lunch**
1 T. sesame oil	**Day One**
6 T. vegetable oil	**3 green onions, chopped**
3 T. rice vinegar	**1 T. sesame seeds**
1 (8 oz.) pkg. rice noodles	**1 (11 oz.) can mandarin**
1 head iceberg lettuce,	**oranges, drained**
rinsed and chopped	

In a medium bowl, whisk together brown sugar, soy sauce, sesame oil, 4 tablespoons vegetable oil and rice vinegar. In a medium skillet over medium heat, place remaining 2 tablespoons vegetable oil. Add a few of the rice noodles and cook until puffed. As noodles begin to puff up and soften, remove to a plate and add more noodles to the skillet. When all noodles have been cooked, place noodles in a large bowl. Add chopped lettuce, 2 cups of the leftover cooked chopped chicken* and chopped green onions and toss until fully incorporated. Pour dressing mixture over salad mixture and toss until evenly coated. Sprinkle sesame seeds and drained mandarin oranges over salad and serve.

*Reserve remaining cooked chopped chicken for Dinner and Lunch on Day 3.

Dinner
Day Two:

Cashew Chicken

Makes 4 to 6 servings

4 C. uncooked white rice
1 C. chicken broth
1 (10 3/4 oz.) can cream
of chicken soup
1 (10 3/4 oz.) can cream
of mushroom soup

2 T. soy sauce
Leftover cooked chopped
chicken from Lunch
1 C. cashews

Preheat oven to 400°. In a medium pot, cook rice according to package directions, until tender. Place half of the cooked rice in an airtight container and refrigerate.* In a large saucepan over medium heat, combine chicken broth, cream of chicken soup, cream of mushroom soup and soy sauce. Bring mixture to a boil and stir in all but 2 cups of the cooked chopped chicken.** Stir in remaining half of the cooked rice and cashews. Spread mixture evenly into a 9x13" baking dish. Bake in oven for 20 to 25 minutes, until heated throughout.
*Reserve half of the cooked rice for Dinner on Day 3.
**Reserve 2 cups of the cooked chopped chicken for Lunch on Day 3.

Breakfast
Day Three:

Brown Sugar Oatmeal

Makes 4 servings

3 C. water	1/2 tsp. vanilla
1 C. powdered milk	3 eggs
1 1/2 C. old fashioned oats	4 tsp. butter
1/2 tsp. cinnamon	1 C. milk
1/2 C. raisins	3 T. honey

In a large saucepan over medium high heat, bring water to a boil. In a medium bowl, combine powdered milk, oats and cinnamon. Quickly stir oat mixture into boiling water. Return to a boil, reduce heat and let simmer for 5 to 10 minutes, or until oatmeal reaches desired thickness. Remove from heat and stir in raisins and vanilla. Add eggs, one at a time, beating well after each addition. Mix well and divide oatmeal evenly into four bowls. Top each bowl with 1 teaspoon butter, 1/4 cup milk and a drizzle of honey.

Lunch
Day Three:

Chicken Quesadillas

Makes 4 to 6 servings

Leftover cooked chopped chicken from Dinner Day Two
1 (1 1/4 oz.) env. fajita seasoning
1 T. vegetable oil
2 green bell peppers, chopped

2 red bell peppers, chopped
1 onion, chopped
10 (10") flour tortillas
1 C. shredded Cheddar cheese
1 C. shredded Monterey Jack cheese

Preheat oven to 350°. In a large saucepan over medium heat, combine leftover chopped cooked chicken from Day 2, fajita seasoning, chopped green bell pepper, chopped red bell peppers and chopped onions. Cook for 10 minutes, stirring occasionally, until vegetables are tender. Divide chicken mixture evenly over half of each tortilla. Sprinkle each tortilla with some of the shredded Cheddar cheese and shredded Monterey Jack cheese. Fold each tortilla in half to enclose the filling. Place folded tortillas on a baking sheet and bake in oven for 10 minutes, or until cheese has melted.

Dinner
Day Three:

Easy Salmon & Rice

Makes 4 servings

Leftover baked salmon fillet from Breakfast Day Two
Leftover chopped onions from Breakfast Day Two
1 (14 1/2 oz.) can mixed vegetables, drained
1 tsp. lemon pepper
1 tsp. garlic salt
Leftover cooked rice from Dinner Day Two
1/4 C. dry bread crumbs
Pinch of paprika

Using a fork, flake the leftover salmon fillet from Day 2 into pieces. In a medium bowl, combine flaked salmon, chopped onions, drained mixed vegetables, lemon pepper and garlic salt. Mix well and stir in leftover cooked rice from Day 2. Spread mixture evenly into a 9x13" baking dish. Sprinkle dry bread crumbs and paprika over mixture. Cover baking dish with aluminum foil and bake in oven for 20 to 30 minutes.

Index

Trip 4
Breakfast:
Lunch:
Dinner:

Trip 5
Breakfast:
Lunch:
Dinner:

Trip 6
Breakfast:
Lunch:
Dinner:

Trip 7

Breakfast:

Lunch:

Dinner:

Trip 8

Breakfast:

Lunch:

Dinner:

Trip 9

Breakfast:

Lunch:

Dinner:

Trip 10

Breakfast:

Lunch:

Dinner:

Trip 11

Breakfast:

Lunch:

Dinner:

Trip 12

Breakfast:

Lunch:

Dinner: